THE GREEN KINGDOM

First published in Great Britain in 2025 by
Dorling Kindersley Limited
20 Vauxhall Bridge Road,
London SW1V 2SA

The authorised representative in the EEA is
Dorling Kindersley Verlag GmbH. Arnulfstr. 124,
80636 Munich, Germany

10 9 8 7 6 5 4 3 2 1
001–343089-Mar/2025

A CIP catalogue record for this book is available from the British Library.

ISBN: 978-0-2417-7069-6

Printed and bound in Australia by Griffin Press

www.dk.com

This book was made with Forest Stewardship Council™ certified paper – one small step in DK's commitment to a sustainable future.
Learn more at www.dk.com/uk/information/sustainability

THE GREEN KINGDOM

Cornelia Funke ✿ Tammi Hartung
Illustrated by Melissa Castrillón

For the real Caspia and her mother Juliane,
who were our scouts in Brooklyn.
C. F.

The Lost Summer

The whole summer?

'Come on, Caspia, it's only for eleven weeks!' Dad had said.

But what on earth would she do for eleven weeks without her friends, her things, her bed, her EVERYTHING? Especially for the best eleven weeks of the year! No eating ice cream at The Frozen Lizard, no swimming in the river, no sleepovers at Ellie's!

'You seriously think that's a bad thing?' Laryssa laughed when Caspia told her and Ellie where she would be spending the summer. 'You'll be in Brooklyn! It'll be amazing!'

But Caspia wasn't a city person. She had spent her whole life in Wilmerton, a small town in the north of Maine.

She and Ellie had always made fun of city people, especially tourists from New York, who descended on Wilmerton like locusts as soon as the leaves changed color and said things like: 'Oh look! How authentic!'

Bad luck! That's what it was. Infuriating, summer-devouring bad luck.

'Here!' said Ellie and slid a bracelet onto Caspia's wrist, as they sat by the river together. 'My cousin brought it back from India. I think it's some sort of dried vine. It's meant to protect you from all sorts of things AND bring you good luck.'

Caspia wasn't sure that a bracelet could protect its wearer, or bring good luck, but she promised to wear it anyway.

In the meantime, Dad was annoyingly excited about the fact that he'd be working on a construction site in New York for the summer. 'We'll be working on the tenth floor. Just imagine that! And I'll be able to see Jamaica Bay from the scaffolding!'

Caspia thought that sounded terribly dangerous, but Dad grinned like a little boy.

Mom was also excited. 'This will be the perfect time to finally work on my cookbook,' she said as they were packing their suitcases.

Mom had been wanting to write a cookbook since Caspia

first started school. But she decided to keep that observation to herself. Her grandmother was already making fun of the idea. Six years ago, they had moved into her grandparents' house, which was huge and had a big backyard. But it also came with some major disadvantages. Caspia loved her mother's cooking, even though she sometimes took the experimenting a little too far. And she thought it was a shame that nothing had come of the cookbook yet.

'I signed up for eleven different cooking classes!' Mom announced as she climbed on top of her suitcase to force it shut. 'In Wilmerton even Chinese food is considered an extravagance! But listen to this: *Authentic cuisine of Bali*,' she read out loud, looking at her cell phone's screen. '*The secrets of south Indian cuisine, Ukrainian bean dishes*. I could hardly decide! Aren't you at least a little bit excited, sweetheart?'

No, she wasn't! She wouldn't have minded having to make do without The Frozen Lizard and her friends for a while if they were going on some adventurous journey instead. To Madagascar for example, where Caspia had been wanting to go since she first saw a documentary about lemurs! She had suggested this to her parents many times already. Going on a big summer trip, a family adventure so to speak. And what were they doing instead? Brooklyn!

It was a long drive, but Caspia barely said a word.

'Brooklyn isn't like Manhattan, Caspia,' Mom had reassured her at least half a dozen times. 'Brooklyn is much nicer and quieter.'

Quieter! The street where Dad had rented an Airbnb was swarming with people and cars. The building where their apartment was looked rather old and the elevator was broken, so that they had to drag their suitcases up four whole flights of stairs. And just because Dad's clumsy friend had dropped a bunch of bricks on his own foot and now needed help on the construction site! Yes, the whole thing was definitely absolutely appallingly bad luck, Caspia thought, as she pushed Ellie's bracelet under her sleeve and dragged her suitcase up the next step.

'Here we are!' said Dad, when he finally used the bent key that the apartment's owner had sent him, to unlock the apartment door. 'It's nice, isn't it?'

Caspia exchanged a quick look with Mom. Flowered wallpaper! Pillows with flowers. Even the rugs had floral patterns on them. The whole apartment looked like the house of Laryssa's grandmother, who was always proudly telling everyone that she used to be a hippie in her day. Meaning: a hundred years ago.

'The woman who rents out the apartment hasn't had

a chance to renovate it yet since her mother passed,' Dad explained when he saw their faces. 'That's why it's a bit old-fashioned.'

'She died?' Caspia threw him a horrified look. 'But not here, right?'

'We got lucky to find anything at all on such short notice, Caspia!' Dad replied. 'Okay, it has a bit of a Mary Poppins feel to it. But it could be worse!'

More like *Little House on the Prairie*, Caspia thought. In Brooklyn.

'The kitchen is great,' said Mom. 'And we can just put away some of the pillows. We'll be fine!'

That evening she announced how much she loved the grocery stores in the area, and Dad raved about all the cool buildings he'd already seen, and how much more exciting it would be to work on a construction site in New York, instead of Wilmerton where there were no houses with more than two stories.

How could the two of them be such traitors?

Three months. Away from everything she knew...

The first night was bad. Dad had neglected to make sure that their apartment had air conditioning, and her room was so hot that Caspia opened the window, just to realize that outside was the exact same temperature. And besides, so much noise was drifting up from the street below that she couldn't sleep anyway and eventually gave up on it entirely.

There was only one spot in her room where the internet worked properly—on the windowsill. So, she crouched down on it and texted Laryssa and Ellie, hoping they were still up. After all, it was only 9:30pm on a Friday night. But the two of them were either asleep already or out. Laryssa often spent the weekends with her cousins, and Ellie spent hers with the Wilmerton Greenlings—who Caspia's grandmother considered to be communists ever since they organized a protest against the new shopping mall that was supposed to be built on the green next to the river.

When she didn't get a response, Caspia set her phone aside. Three months! She closed her fingers around the small ceramic fish that she wore on a string around her neck. Laryssa and Ellie had the same one. They had bought them in a shop in Wilmerton, to celebrate that they had been friends for seven years. That was more than half their lives. Three months! Should she make a calendar where she could cross off the days? No, that would only remind her how many were left. Maybe she should leave her things in her bag, so it felt more like they were about to go home again soon. She sighed once more and looked over at her suitcase. *No, Caspia*, she told herself. *Unless you want to be the smalltown girl from Maine walking around Brooklyn in crumpled T-shirts*. She could only hope that people here would not be as mean to her as she and Ellie were to tourists from New York...

Underneath the window was a large, old dresser. Maybe she should put her things in there. It was actually pretty nice. Of course it was also covered in flowers. But these looked as if someone had painted them on themself, someone who had tried to depict real flowers, even though Caspia had no idea which ones. She had never paid much attention to plants, except for the poison ivy that grew by the river.

She ran her fingers over the painted flowers and leaves. She could feel brushstrokes. Yes, somebody really had painted them by hand.

The top drawer required a strong jolt to open. But she was used to that from her grandmother's old dresser. Surprise! The drawer was lined with faded floral paper. Caspia covered it with her T-shirts and underwear. In the second one she found room for her jeans, socks, and all of the sweaters she had brought because she was used to cool Maine weather. Would it stay this warm? How did people accomplish anything in this heat?

The bottom drawer was even more stuck than the others, and Caspia was just about to give up when it finally budged. That hadn't been easy. A bundle of letters was sitting on the floral paper—as if it had been unwedged from behind the drawer when she opened it.

Letters... Which seemed as old-fashioned as the wallpaper. One of her great aunts still sent birthday cards in envelopes. But Caspia couldn't think of any other letter she had ever opened or even held in her hands.

The envelopes were long and narrow and made from pale-green linen paper. Someone had tied them together with a green velvet ribbon and carefully placed a dried flower underneath the bow. It was violet blue.

Caspia took the bundle from the drawer. It looked as if the letters had been very important to someone. Maybe the old lady who had lived here. It would probably be best to tell the woman renting out the apartment about them. But the letters looked so inviting. As if they were whispering: *Caspia, come on. Read us! We've been waiting for you.*

Were they love letters? In movies they usually were.

Caspia took a picture to send to Ellie and Laryssa.

The violet flower fell into her lap when she untied the ribbon, and the envelopes felt as if they could hardly wait to reveal the words that were hidden inside. There were ten letters, and they had all been opened before. The handwriting on the envelopes was swirly and old-fashioned. Caspia could barely decipher it.

The recipient was always the same.

Minna Reynolds
2101 Beekman Place #5c
Brooklyn, NY
USA

That was the address of their apartment. But the address of the sender was different on each letter. Caspia did not even know where some of the places were, but she knew the countries: China, Egypt, Scotland... Yes, the letters came from all over, but only one person had sent them.

Rosalind Reynolds.

Caspia hesitated and ran her fingers over the first envelope. What harm could it really do if she read one of the letters? Dad could still give them to the owner afterwards.

She opened the first envelope and pulled out the letter, which had been carefully folded to fit inside perfectly. The paper was the same pale green as the envelope, and the handwriting on it was also the same.

Dear Sister,

Here is my first riddle! So we can travel together even though you are so far away. As promised, the plants that you will have to guess will not be very rare nor unknown to you. Also, each one will have a connection to the human world.

Can you imagine, Minna, Papa and I are quite the celebrities by now! The British botanist and his blind daughter who travel the world together, to explore the Green Kingdom. I make all the gardeners rather nervous when I touch their plants with my fingers to get to know them! But I think the plants like it! So...as agreed, here are your five clues that will help you guess the answer.

Caspia stared down at the letter in her hand, while the night outside was still filled with voices and car noise. There was a date in the top right corner: March 27, 1958. Her mom had not even been born then. But the words on the pale-green paper...they were so alive. They sounded as if someone had reached for her hand.

'Hi, Rosalind!' she said quietly. 'It's a pleasure to meet you.'

No, she would not return these letters. Not yet.

Rosalind's First Letter

March 27, 1958

Dear Sister,

Here is my first riddle! So we can travel together even though you are so far away. As promised, the plants that you will have to guess will not be very rare nor unknown to you. Also, each one will have a connection to the human world.

Can you imagine, Minna, Papa and I are quite the celebrities by now! The British botanist and his blind daughter, who travel the world together, to explore the Green Kingdom. I make all the gardeners rather nervous when I touch their plants with my fingers to get to know them! But I think the plants like it! So…as agreed, here are your five clues that will help you guess the answer.

1. Humans have been stealing the skin of this tree for thousands of years.

2. It is home to the purple-faced langur monkey and 45 different species of lizard.

3. It serves cooks and bakers alike—and cures a fever!

4. This is my favorite clue: this tree is said to be guarded by venomous flying serpents!

'Rosalind!' I hear you sigh. 'This is too difficult. There are more than 73,000 tree species on this planet!'

All right. Here is one last clue:

5. It is hot and humid where Papa and I are at the moment! This tree does not like the cold at all.

So... Which citizen of the Green Kingdom is it?

I suggest that you take that embroidery needle, Minna, and the thread with which you have enchanted my fingers so many times before. Embroider a portrait of the plant described in my riddle and send it to me! If it feels familiar to my hands, I will send you the next riddle.

But for now, I am sending you a fierce hug!

From your little sister,
Rosalind

PS: Papa has kindly agreed to write out these letters for me as I dictate them. I am sure you have recognized his handwriting already. So he will be a part of our game as well, which I thought you would like.

The Spice Shop

'It's actually not so bad here,' Caspia said over breakfast.

Her parents exchanged a surprised look. That morning the caretaker had announced that the elevator was finally fixed. But Mom had gotten stuck in it anyway, after going to buy croissants at the bakery next door. She had been a little less enthused about their Brooklyn adventure ever since.

'Do you guys know which tree humans steal the skin from?' Caspia asked.

Another confused look.

'Cork is made from tree bark... I think,' said Dad. 'But I have no idea which tree.'

'This bark can also be used for cooking and baking,"

Caspia said, as she poured herself a glass of orange juice. Come to think of it, did oranges grow on bushes or on trees?

She still had not sent the picture of the letters to Ellie and Laryssa. She had also taken one of the first riddle, but what if they thought it was strange that she found the ancient letters of a plant-loving girl to her sister so fascinating? Ellie would probably understand, but she wasn't so sure about Laryssa.

Mom had printed out the schedule for her cooking classes and was frowning at it. 'Is that question with the tree for a piece of homework you got over the summer?'

'No. Just a riddle someone posted,' Caspia replied evasively. That was not really a lie, was it? Rosalind had just posted it in a very old-fashioned way.

She hadn't had any luck when she googled the tree skin. But maybe the clue with the purple-faced langur monkeys and the lizards would be more helpful. Maybe in combination with the stolen bark? There... Yes! That might be the right answer!

'Cinnamon!' Caspia mumbled. 'I had no idea that cinnamon is actually tree bark.'

'No cell phones at breakfast!' Mom said. 'That rule also applies in Brooklyn.'

'I have to run.' Dad got up and gave Mom a kiss goodbye.

'Sorry, but I don't want to be late on my very first day. But I like talking about trees at breakfast! Of course! After all, you can build boats from them.'

Dad loved boats. At home he spent hours building model ships in the evenings. And the paper boats that he used to make for Caspia's bathtime when she was little had always floated exceptionally well. Maybe that trip to the Amazon would happen one day after all. Even though Dad contented himself with looking down on the water from scaffolding this summer.

'I think I got a little over-excited booking these cooking courses,' Mom mumbled. 'I underestimated how long it would take to get everywhere. The classes are spread out all over Brooklyn!'

Caspia was very tempted to tell her about the letters. But she was still worried that Mom would want to give them to the landlady right away. And she really wanted to know if Minna had solved the riddle and if cinnamon was indeed the right answer.

'Oh well!' Mom set the list aside. 'The first course doesn't start until tomorrow. Maybe I'll come up with some new recipes today!'

She had come up with countless recipes over the last few years and tested them all out on Caspia and her dad with varying degrees of success. But Grandma liked to make fun of the fact that her daughter dreamed of putting all her experiments into a cookbook. 'I've also been a good cook my whole life!' she would say. 'But that doesn't mean I think I can write books.' For Grandma there were only three types of people who had sensible jobs: teachers, bankers, and lawyers. Which definitely did not include Dad, who had not even gone to college. And not Mom, who had left college early to have a daughter named Caspia. No, writing cookbooks was not something that Grandma considered real work. But Grandma wasn't here, and maybe this time Mom would really sit down and work on her dream.

When her mother disappeared into the kitchen, Caspia took the rest of her breakfast back to her room. The dresser was an excellent scouting point, so Caspia put her plate and her glass down on the dark wood and pulled herself up next to them and looked down into the cul-de-sac outside their apartment building. On the right somebody had painted a garden onto the wall that separated the houses from the rail tracks that ran behind them. On the left, the small street opened up onto Flatbush Avenue where masses of pedestrians, dogs, bicycles, and cars rushed past day and night. So many people, so many windows, so many stories...like those in Rosalind's letters.

Since Caspia found out about her and Minna, the floral wallpaper actually looked kind of nice. Even though she could not name a single one of the flowers on it, just as she couldn't name a single one of the plants on the dresser. They weren't roses, those she knew from her grandparents' backyard. Grandma loved roses. They were the only flowers she allowed there.

A bird flew by the window, and right in front of the glass pane a spider spun her web. Clouds drifted through the sky above the roofs, which made it look like a herd of sheep was grazing on an endless blue meadow. Maybe living on the fifth floor for a while wasn't so bad after all.

Was it really a cinnamon tree that Rosalind had written about? Caspia climbed off the dresser and took the first letter out of the drawer once more. Rosalind's words were so vivid, they held the entire world in them. Caspia read the address on the envelope. Anuradhapura. Ceylon. Wasn't that modern-day Sri Lanka? Yes, that fit. Cinnamon trees grew in Sri Lanka on huge plantations.

If Minna had come to the same conclusion...

Caspia compared the photos that her phone showed her of cinnamon trees with the plants that had been painted onto the dresser. There! A branch on the first drawer definitely looked like it belonged to a cinnamon tree. So, Minna had come up with the same answer, and she had not only embroidered the solution to Rosalind's riddle but had also painted it onto her dresser. Yes, that's what must have happened. Caspia closed her eyes and imagined hearing the chattering of purple-faced langur monkeys. For a moment she imagined that the large drawers were filled with forests and jungles and that she could climb inside and find Rosalind there. *And your socks and underwear, Caspia!*

She climbed up on the dresser once more and looked down on the human-built jungle. Ping! A huge question mark appeared on her cell phone.

Stolen tree skin? What are you doing? I thought you were in Brooklyn?

Laryssa. Of course. She had seen the pictures of the stack of letters and Rosalind's first riddle. Caspia had sent them after all. She missed Ellie and Laryssa, even though Laryssa could be really annoying. Caspia had a suspicion that she even enjoyed being annoying at times.

No, I am in Anuradhapura, she wrote back. And I think the answer is: cinnamon tree.

You are in the most exciting city in the world! Laryssa responded. Who cares about tree riddles? Send us pictures of the people!

I like the clue with the flying serpents. That

was Ellie. Her mind often worked in similar ways to Caspia's.

Maybe my bracelet made you open that drawer, she wrote. **Maybe it even magically summoned those letters.**

Well...sometimes Ellie believed pretty strange things. And she definitely had too high an opinion of amulets and bracelets. But nobody was perfect.

Caspia set aside her phone and looked out the window once more. It seemed unlikely that there would be any cinnamon trees in Brooklyn. But surely she could buy some ground cinnamon somewhere. And maybe Mom could invent a new recipe with it?

She took the letters out of the drawer and lined them up, until they wound across the carpet like a pale-green road. If she opened one a week, they would last for over two months, making her feel like she was traveling the world with Rosalind and having adventures in wild places, instead of being stuck in Brooklyn. But only one letter a week... Caspia could hardly stop herself from opening the second one now! Maybe a letter every three days was more realistic?

Yes.

Mom was peeling red onions when she went into the kitchen, and as always it was making her cry her eyes out.

Surely onions were plants. Weird that she had never thought about that before.

'Do onions grow under or above ground, Mom?'

Her mother wiped away her tears with a dish towel. Her mascara was smeared all over her face. Dad called this her onion face. 'Underground. But the greens that they grow above ground also taste really good. In college I used to grow onions in a pot on my windowsill. The green part tastes great on cheese and fried eggs. Maybe they're taking their revenge on me for that now!'

Caspia opened the cupboard where Mom had lined up all her spices. She had brought half a suitcase full despite Grandma's comments.

'What are you looking for?' She wiped her eyes one more time and reached for a frying pan.

'Cinnamon.' Caspia's eyes roamed across the glass jars. Other mothers loved buying dresses and shoes. Her mother bought spices. Paprika, cayenne pepper, tarragon... Those were probably also all plants...

Mom leaned across Caspia's shoulder and reached for a jar that only contained the smallest trace of red-brown powder. 'Sorry, but there's a spice shop right around the corner.'

Caspia sniffed the empty jar. It still held a slight murmur

of cinnamon inside. And of monkeys and lizards... Scents whisked you away on journeys so easily.

Caspia's clothes still smelled like Maine. Just like Mom's.

'Okay, I'll go and buy cinnamon and you'll invent a new recipe. But nothing too out there!'

'I have no idea what you're talking about!' Mom said and smiled mischievously. She loved adventure-cooking as she called it. Ellie had a theory that Mom had been an alchemist in a former life.

'No, no, I was a witch, Ellie,' was Mom's response to this. 'A witch who found herbal remedies in the woods! With a talent for cooking. So all my potions tasted delicious!'

She could be very funny sometimes. But Ellie had been a bit nervous around Mom for a while after this.

It was warm outside, the sort of warmth that you only got in Wilmerton once every ten years, and Caspia regretted her habit of always taking a jacket as she merged into the throng of strangers on the sidewalk. So many faces. At home everyone looked the same somehow—as if they were all made from the same clay. Wilmerton played the same melody every day. But Brooklyn struck Caspia as a wild symphony, played by thousands of human instruments. But somehow all the sounds came together in harmony.

Nobody looked Caspia up and down with a 'where-did-you-come-from?' look like she had feared. Nobody seemed to really care where she came from. Everybody was busy with their own affairs. Which actually felt kind of nice. No '*Mrs Persimmons complained that you didn't say hello to her when you ran into her at the store. Oh well, you know what she's like*.' Yes, she did know. It felt so different walking down the street where nobody knew you. Different in a good, but also bad, way. And it scared her a little to be surrounded by so many strangers.

The spice shop was right across from the newsstand that Dad had raved about. The narrow façade was a bright shade of red—at home their neighbors had complained because Mom had painted their front door in almost the same color. When Caspia stopped in front of the shop window, her reflection filled up with glass jars, baskets, and colorful ceramic bowls. All the powders, seeds, fruits, and dried leaves they contained really did make you think of a witch's store. Ellie would have been fascinated and intimidated at the same time. And Laryssa would have been annoyed by how horribly messy the store was.

A chain with small copper bells rang out when Caspia opened the door, and a thousand different scents welcomed her. Dark wooden shelves reached all the way up to the ceiling, filled with glass jars, cans, and other containers in all shapes and sizes. Between the baskets on the counter stood a wooden figure with many arms, which Caspia assumed must depict a deity. And on the old-fashioned cash register, a small golden dragon spread its wings.

'Welcome.' A tiny woman rose from a chair next to the counter. Her hair was gray and Caspia suspected that she was at least a hundred years old. (She found out later that Mrs Wahid was actually only eighty-one.) She was dressed in Western clothes with wide, black pants and a red shirt, but she was wearing a dozen exotic-looking bracelets and many rings on her fingers.

'Hello,' Caspia said shyly. 'Do you happen to have any...'

She froze.

A tiny dog shot out from underneath the chair and barked at her so ferociously that he lifted off the ground a little bit with each bark. He had a face like a monkey and was spotted like a leopard.

'Diam, Monyet!' The old woman shooed the dog back under the chair.

'I am so sorry, he thinks he has to protect me from every single person who comes into the store. May I ask what your name is?'

'Caspia,' she mumbled as her eyes wandered over more

dragons on the shelves as well as another few multi-armed gods. 'Caspia Turkel.'

The old woman nodded as if that was all she needed to know about Caspia. 'I am Mrs Wahid,' she said as she stepped behind the counter. 'What can I do for you? Did your mother send you?'

'No, but I think she has been here before,' Caspia said. 'Short black hair? Slight Maine accent?'

'Oh yes!' Mrs Wahid smiled. 'You look a lot like her. She picked out some very interesting spices. Is she a good cook?'

'Yes. Very good actually. But sometimes she experiments a little too much.'

She picked out some very interesting spices. That sounded a bit disconcerting.

The golden dragon on the register looked so beautiful. Caspia wanted to run her fingers over the spikes on his back. But she heard her grandmother's voice in her head. *Don't touch things that don't belong to you, Caspia!* Grandma always grabbed her hand when she attempted it anyway. Rosalind would not have liked that one bit. After all, she experienced the world through her hands.

'You can touch him!' Mrs Wahid seemed to have read her thoughts. 'Touching a dragon is good luck! And then you can tell me what you would like to buy.'

Caspia slowly let her fingers run over the golden spikes. The metal felt smooth as though it had been polished by many fingers.

'Cinnamon. I am looking for cinnamon. Do you have any?'

Mrs Wahid laughed. Her laughter sounded like that of a bird. She even looked a little like one, with her large dark eyes and the fine gray hair that covered her head like down.

'Do I have cinnamon? You are talking about one of the most important spices in the world, my heart. Are you looking for Chinese cinnamon or for Ceylon cinnamon? Would you prefer sticks, leaves, or powder? Or maybe it'd be better if I asked what you'd like to use it for? For drinking, seasoning, cooking, healing?'

'Sticks, I think,' Caspia replied. 'But leaves would also be wonderful.'

She was a little dizzy from all the scents that surrounded her, but in a good way. As if she was in a thousand places at once.

Mrs Wahid shook her head regretfully. 'Unfortunately, I don't have any cinnamon leaves at the moment. But I am sure we can find cinnamon sticks and powder. Excuse my curiosity, but why cinnamon?'

When she smiled, countless small wrinkles showed

up around her eyes—evidence that Mrs Wahid smiled very often.

'I found a bundle of old letters.' Caspia pulled her phone out of her pocket to show Mrs Wahid the photos she had taken of them.

Mrs Wahid fished a pair of glasses out of the drawer in the counter and put them on her nose.

'A green riddle!' she murmured. 'How exciting. And her sister was called Minna?'

She gave the cell phone back to Caspia. 'I think I knew her. She used to come here to buy spiced hot chocolate. But I didn't know that she had a sister who sent her green riddles! Well then... Let's find your cinnamon!'

She climbed up a tall ladder that looked so old it made Caspia a little nervous. But Mrs Wahid did not just look like a bird. She seemed to be very comfortable in those airy heights and she was as light-footed as a robin climbing up and down the ladder. She collected three jars off the top shelf and put one after the other on the counter.

The first contained a red-orange powder, the second long brown sticks, and the third something that looked like thin sheets of brown paper. Mrs Wahid got three small paper bags from her drawer and filled each with the content of one of the jars.

'There you go,' she said, as she pushed the small bags across the counter to Caspia. 'I am intrigued to hear which cinnamon you and your mother liked best.'

Caspia gave the bags a worried look. 'Maybe I better only take one. I don't have a lot of money with me.'

How much was a spice that came from so far away? Surely a lot!

But Mrs Wahid just shook her head, smiling. 'They are yours for just one dollar. Consider it my payment to you for telling me the story of Minna's sister and her riddles.'

One dollar. That really wasn't too much. Caspia put the bill in Mrs Wahid's narrow, bejeweled hand. 'Do you mind if I take a picture of your store for my friends back home?'

'And where is that?' Mrs Wahid asked with a wink.

'Wilmerton, Maine. We are only here for the summer vacation. Me and my parents.'

'So three months!' Mrs Wahid smiled. 'That will give you enough time to get to know Brooklyn a little better. And hopefully discover a few things that you will enjoy remembering when you are back home. Take as many photos as you wish.'

Caspia took quite a lot, while Mrs Wahid sat back down on her chair. Then she put the three small paper bags in the basket that she had found in Minna's kitchen, waved at Mrs

Wahid one more time, and, with a final glance at the golden dragon, walked toward the shop door. The tiny dog barked after her but stayed under the chair.

'Mrs Wahid, what is the name of your dog?' Caspia asked, before she stepped back outside.

'Oh, this is Monyet.' Mrs Wahid gently stroked his small head. 'That's actually the name of a cheeky little monkey in Indonesia, my former home. Come back soon and tell me which cinnamon you liked best. And I'd love to hear another one of Minna's sister's green riddles.'

'Promise!' Caspia responded.

She stepped back out onto the sidewalk almost unwillingly. She could have stayed in Mrs Wahid's spice shop for hours. Maybe...

Caspia turned around and opened the shop door one more time, despite the risk of Monyet barking at her again.

'Do you know if there is a cinnamon tree somewhere in Brooklyn, Mrs Wahid?' she asked into the ringing of the small bells and Monyet's growling.

'Why don't you try the Botanic Garden?' Mrs Wahid looked up from the magazine she had started reading. 'It is a wonderful place. And even if you don't find a cinnamon tree there, you are sure to meet many other interesting trees. And it is just a short walk from here.'

The Brooklyn Botanic Garden... As soon as Caspia was back on the sidewalk, she checked on her cell phone to see where it was. Mrs Wahid had been right. The BBG was only a short walk away, and the way there really didn't look complicated at all.

I have the cinnamon, but I'm going for a walk. I'll be back soon, she wrote to Mom. She always told her parents where she was, even though she was almost thirteen. Laryssa made fun of her for that. But after all, Mom and Dad always let her know where she could reach them. They were a team! *Can you ask your parents if they'll adopt me?* Laryssa had asked once. *You are so lucky, Caspia Turkel! Your parents let you be yourself. They don't constantly try to turn you into the daughter they decided you should be before you were even born.*

Caspia reviewed the route she'd have to take one more time.

Ping. Have you found any serpents yet? Ellie asked. I hope the bracelet is protecting you?

It is, Caspia replied. So far only tiny barking dogs, no flying serpents yet. But that could change as soon as I'm at the Botanic Garden. IF they have a cinnamon tree there.

She liked the confused emoji Ellie sent back.

Cinnamon

The Garden

'Welcome to the Brooklyn Botanic Garden!' The voice of the woman behind the ticket counter matched her bright red hair. She was wearing a T-shirt with the BBG's logo on it. 'You're coming at the exact right time, my dear! Our summer flowers are in full bloom!'

Caspia had no idea which flowers those would be, but she hid her ignorance behind a smile.

'Could you tell me if there's a cinnamon tree here, Ms...' She glanced at the name tag that dangled off a chain just above the logo. '... Wood?'

'Call me Margaret, my dear,' replied the woman as she perused her computer screen. 'Cinnamon tree,' she mumbled with a frown. 'Cinammomum? No, wait! Cinnamomum of course! I always forget how to spell it.'

She smiled at Caspia with coral red lips. 'Yes, we have the Chinese variety. *Cinnamomum cassia*. Tropical pavilion. Do you know how to get there?'

Caspia shook her head.

Margaret pulled a visitor map from a stand next to her and unfolded it. Each one of her red fingernails was decorated with a tiny white flower. Laryssa would definitely have asked where she could have that done herself.

'We are here, my dear.' Margaret put her flower finger on the map. 'And you just follow this path... You can't miss the greenhouse.'

Our summer flowers are in full bloom. Whatever they were called, they were spectacular and everywhere. Plants definitely came in many more colors and shapes than people! Caspia was very tempted to pick a bouquet, but she was fairly sure that if she did Margaret would not greet her quite so warmly at her next visit. And it was clear to Caspia that she would want to come back here a lot. It soothed the country girl in her to be surrounded by trees and flowers. The air tasted fresher, and the world felt so much wider and freer than it did between buildings.

Margaret was right. The tropical pavilion was impossible

to miss. Caspia had never been in such a large greenhouse before. So many trees and flowers underneath a sky of glass! Very different from the small plastic greenhouse where her neighbor used to grow his tomatoes.

The air was so damp and warm that Caspia would not have been surprised if flowers had started to sprout on her skin. Did plants like to live this sheltered? Or would they have preferred to grow in the wilderness. *Maybe they're like people*, she thought she could hear Rosalind say. *Some like the open sky, while others prefer a house of glass.*

Maybe...

According to the signs, all the plants here came from far away. *Green immigrants*, Caspia thought, *who have to make Brooklyn their home now*. Where did the palm tree she was passing consider home? Was that always the place where you were born? Or could you put down new roots? The plants that surrounded her had done it—but could the new roots ever be as strong as the old ones?

It didn't take Caspia long to find the cinnamon tree that Margaret had looked up on her computer. 'Chinese Cinnamon Tree / *Cinnamomum cassia* Origin: Sri Lanka,' the sign next to it announced. A few steps further was a larger sign explaining the use of the bark and how long and for what purpose cinnamon had been used by humans.

Cinnamomum cassia—why do plants have scientific names? Caspia texted Ellie. Ellie loved to find out information like this.

The cinnamon tree in Brooklyn still had its brown bark. Nobody had peeled strips of skin off its trunk with a sharp, curved knife. But its leaves seemed to whisper of the faraway island it came from. It was still pretty small compared to the trees Caspia had seen on her phone. Unfortunately, none of the flying serpents had accompanied it to Brooklyn, and none of the purple-faced monkeys or even a few of the lizards that Caspia had read about. Did the cinnamon tree miss them? Did they somehow belong there, all the animals that lived as part of it?

The tree was not directly on the paved path and she would have to stretch pretty far to be able to touch it. But she had to try. Caspia looked around. Good, she seemed to be the only visitor in the tropical greenhouse that morning. She closed her eyes, leaned forward, and stretched her hand out for the bark that did not only taste good but could also heal people. It was both smooth and rough at the same time—it felt so different from human skin. Did it cause the cinnamon tree pain when they cut its skin with sharp knives, to harvest it? Did it bleed?

'You're lucky, Brooklyn cinnamon!' Caspia whispered. 'Believe me! Even though you probably miss the monkeys and lizards. And it probably annoys you that you can't grow as tall because of the glass roof.'

She picked up one of the leaves that lay on the asphalt beneath the tree. Yes! It smelled of cinnamon when she squeezed it between her fingers.

Just imagine, Rosalind, she thought. *I actually managed to find a cinnamon tree in Brooklyn! Maybe it came here as reluctantly as I did. But... We're making our way!*

Had it already been here when Minna was alive? Caspia looked up at the tree. How quickly did a cinnamon tree grow? Rosalind would probably have known how old this one was. Caspia took a step back and took a few pictures for Ellie and Laryssa.

No serpents or monkeys! she told them. **But the tree is really beautiful.**

Looks like you're in a glass palace, Laryssa sent back. **Who's the boy?**

The boy?

Caspia looked at the photo she had just taken—feeling caught, she looked past the tree.

Yes, a few steps away there was a boy. He didn't seem to have noticed her either. He was holding a notepad and appeared to be drawing something.

Go and introduce yourself! Laryssa texted.

Typical. That's what Laryssa would have done, of course. But Caspia did not just go up to boys she didn't know! Not in Maine and not in Brooklyn.

I think he's drawing something, Ellie wrote.

Yes. A bush with huge trumpet flowers. When he looked up from his notepad, Caspia retreated further behind the cinnamon tree. Good thing Laryssa couldn't see her! The cinnamon tree understood. It hid her with its trunk and its leaves and didn't mock her for her shyness. Caspia was starting to appreciate that about plants: how they enveloped you in their scent and in the beauty of their flowers, provided shade, seasoned food, and, just like her, had come here from faraway places.

Maybe Ellie was right after all. Maybe the bracelet she'd given Caspia was good luck and had made her find Rosalind's letters. It didn't really matter. The important thing was that she had found them.

Caspia put her phone in the basket with Mrs Wahid's small paper bags and looked through the branches of the cinnamon tree once more. But the boy was gone. As if he'd only been a ghost who emerged from one of the large trumpet flowers he had been drawing.

Mom was still adventure-cooking when Caspia got back.

'How was your walk?'

'There's a botanic garden not far from here.'

Mom threw her a quick glance. 'You're still upset with us for making you come to the city, aren't you?'

Was she? Caspia wasn't so sure what she thought about it anymore. 'It's all right,' she said, as she lined up the three cinnamon bags. 'Mrs Wahid wants to know which cinnamon we like the best. Oh and—she remembered you and says I look like you.'

'Everybody thinks that, but you actually look a lot more like your dad!'

Mom was the only one who thought that.

Caspia opened the bag with the cinnamon sticks. The scent that emerged from it was like taking a ride on Mrs Wahid's golden dragon. She tried to imagine Rosalind stepping into her store—and realized that she always pictured Rosalind in some long, old-fashioned gown. *No, Caspia*, she chided herself, *Rosalind didn't send those letters to Minna two hundred years ago. She sent them in 1958!*

What did people wear back then? That was a question for Laryssa.

What Caspia had christened cinnamon paper smelled just as good as the powder. But Mom agreed with her that the sticks had the most cinnamony smell. And that they—surprisingly—inspired her to cook a mushroom dish.

'Yes, a cinnamony wild mushroom ragout! That reminds you that cinnamon trees can also grow in wild forests. What do you think?'

Caspia thought that sounded very promising. And the dish that filled the kitchen with its woody cinnamon scent met her expectations completely. It tasted like an adventure—an adventure that had been seasoned by Rosalind's letter and Mrs Wahid's store. But before she devoured the steaming food that Mom put down on the table—almost forgetting to leave some for Dad!—Caspia took a picture for Laryssa and Ellie. And even though she couldn't include the cinnamon scent, the emojis that came back were full of envy.

Caspia could still taste the cinnamon on her tongue when Laryssa sent pictures of women's fashion from 1958. Plenty of skirts but no jeans at all. Grandma would have liked that. She often complained that Caspia did not wear enough dresses. Ellie found out that people have been giving scientific names to plants for about 300 years. Caspia suspected that the Swedish naturalist who had first come up with the idea had grown tired of the fact that the exact same plant could sometimes have hundreds of different names, even in the same country.

Caspia slept very well that night. Not even the noise that wafted over from Flatbush Avenue bothered her—even though she would have loved to sleep under the cinnamon tree, with nothing but the glass roof and the stars above her. Or at least the few stars you could see over Brooklyn at night. Between all the lights it was easy to forget about the rest of the universe.

Rosalind's Second Letter

May 2, 1958

Dearest Minna,

I love your stitched portrait of the cinnamon tree. Especially the monkey that you added in! And the three lizards! I could feel all of their scales. You are a sculptress with needle and thread.

And as your reward, here is the second riddle:

1. This plant is a world traveler and her preferred mode of transportation is the parachute.

2. European settlers brought the seeds to America so that the flowers could feed their bees.

3. In some languages, this plant has sharp teeth.

4. The young leaves are delicious and strengthen muscles and bones.

5. When you rub the leaves onto your skin, it supposedly makes your dreams come true. Some even claim that you can summon the dead this way.

Are these not fascinating clues, Minna? And I am absolutely certain that this plant grows even in Brooklyn.

Embroider its portrait for me, and once you guess right, I will send you the next riddle.

I send you a garden full of love!
Rosalind

Lions' Teeth

The first clue was the most helpful. And the third. After all, not many plants have sharp teeth in their name. Yes. That, put together with the parachute...the answer to Rosalind's riddle was without a doubt DANDELION! *Löwenzahn* in German and according to Google *dente di leone* in Italian. Which both translated to Lion's Tooth. Ellie, who was completely thrilled about Rosalind's green riddles at this point, found out that its snappy name had in fact nothing at all to do with teeth or lions, but referred to the mighty bite of the sun—and the fact that the blossoms of the dandelion resembled it so much.

Caspia had to admit that the solution to the second riddle disappointed her a little bit. She had hoped for another exotic plant. But dandelion? Even Caspia was very familiar with this one, since Mr Jacobs, her neighbor in Maine, had declared war on it. Mr Jacobs dug up every dandelion that dared to grow on his lawn with an expression so grim it made you think the yellow blossom was ringing in the end of the world. And he called the plant that Rosalind obviously liked very much *stink weed* or *yellow plague*. One time he even bought poison to drive out the plant once and for all—until Mom gave him a lecture about how he was also killing birds and insects with it. Since then, Mr Jacobs pointedly chucked all of his dug-up dandelions over the fence and onto Grandma's rose beds.

Clue number four fit as well. Young dandelion leaves were not only tasty, but also very nutritious because they contained a lot of calcium and potassium. Caspia doubted that Mr Jacobs knew that. Ellie of course wanted to try out the fifth clue right away and head straight to the Wilmerton cemetery to look for dandelions and find out who could be summoned by their leaves. Caspia closed the chat when Ellie and Laryssa started to plan this endeavor in earnest. The time had come to see if Rosalind had been right and if it really was easy to find lions' teeth in Brooklyn.

It was raining when she set out and soon it poured so hard that Caspia was dodging umbrellas left and right.

She should have listened to Mom and brought one herself. But the elevator was still stuck, and she hadn't been able to muster the energy to walk all the way back up to the fifth floor. So she held Minna's basket up over her head as she scoured the sidewalk for yellow flowers that resembled small suns.

For a moment she was tempted to drop in on Mrs Wahid. Her store was probably warm and cozy! But Laryssa and Ellie had fully committed to solving Rosalind's riddles, and it would be really embarrassing if they were the first to send a picture of a dandelion.

They had not been able to find any cinnamon trees in Maine.

Subway tickets, to-go cups, fast-food bags, cigarette butts ... Caspia had much preferred the flowery paths of the Botanic Garden over searching the streets of Brooklyn for a plant that didn't even reach her knees. Still. She was surprised by how many brave plants sprouted by the house fronts or from gaps in the tarmac. Some even appeared to be tiny young trees. Soon she was so absorbed in her search that she ran into more and more people.

'Are you blind, girl?' snapped a man, whose frown reminded her of Mr Jacobs.

No, Caspia thought as she kept her eyes strained on the

sidewalk. *I'm just solving the riddle of a blind girl.*

Ping. Ellie sent a picture of a meadow covered in dandelions. Great.

Dandelion! Where are you? Come on! No way could this be more difficult than the cinnamon tree!

It had stopped raining and the sun was turning the puddles on the sidewalk into liquid silver. But still no *dente di leone*. *You were wrong, Rosalind!* Caspia thought, as she turned the next corner. *There is not a single dandelion in Brooklyn!*

And just then...as if *Taraxacum officinale*—its scientific name—had heard her... Caspia spotted a golden blossom that was proudly reaching its face toward the sun outside a parking lot fence.

'Hello, *Taraxacum*!' Caspia whispered and knelt down on the sidewalk despite the rain. 'I am so, so happy to find you here!'

She closed her eyes and ran her fingers over the long leaves. So different from the bark of the cinnamon tree. The slender stem was firm and smooth and carried the large blossom, apparently without any effort at all.

Ping. Laryssa had found a dandelion next to the entrance of a supermarket.

Imagine if people were as varied as plants! Ellie texted.

Some small and green, others giant with wooden skin. Wouldn't that be fantastic?

And a little scary, Caspia thought, as she pictured these tree people stomping down the street.

That the dandelion was still proudly standing there, despite all the feet and bicycles, proved in an impressive way how resilient it was. Let alone all the dogs... Monyet would surely have peed on the flower!

Caspia got up and took a picture of the brave Brooklyn dandelion. Was it different from its relatives in Maine, just as a city person was different from someone living in a small town? Caspia discovered another dandelion behind an empty can. This one had already grown small parachute seeds on its stem. What if... ? Yes! It was probably not a good idea to eat the leaves with all the car exhaust fumes that must have collected on them. But maybe she could try to grow some little dandelion plants herself?

Carefully she plucked off some of the fluffy seeds and tucked them into her wallet. When she picked the last ones, two of them sailed away, higher and higher, far above the parked cars and toward the strip of blue sky that was poking out between the buildings. The dandelion plants by her feet had probably come here the same way. What an adventurous way of sending your children out into the world. For a moment Caspia pictured her parents putting her up on the windowsill and strapping a parachute to her back. 'Good luck, Caspia!' Then a gentle nudge and she would soar high up into the sky, surrounded by hundreds of other children, whose parents had sent them out into the world in the same way, to find a place where they could grow flowers and roots.

I definitely would not have picked Brooklyn as my place to land, Caspia thought. Although...she had found Rosalind's letters here. And Mrs Wahid. And a cinnamon tree. And a very brave dandelion...all in just a few days!

Caspia bent down and picked up the empty can. It would make a good pot for her plants, and the rain had washed it nice and clean. Now she just needed a little soil without cigarette butts in it and that she could be sure had not been peed on by a dog. Maybe from the Botanic Garden? But that was a long way and the patch of blue sky had already vanished behind dark clouds. No. Caspia had a better idea.

'I didn't expect to see you again so soon!' Mrs Wahid said with her hoarse but happy voice, when Caspia entered the store, accompanied by the gentle sound of bells. 'Is there a cinnamon tree in the Botanic Garden?'

'Yes!' Caspia took a hasty step back when Monyet shot out from underneath Mrs Wahid's chair. But this time he seemed to recognize her and, after a long, disapproving look, turned his tiny pig's tail on her and disappeared back behind his owner's legs.

'I really must apologize for him,' Mrs Wahid said. 'Monyet is getting old and grumpy, and his eyesight is rather poor. Luckily, he still has his nose, otherwise he probably wouldn't even recognize me anymore! So...tell me about the cinnamon tree! Is it big?'

'Not especially. But it is good that way. After all, it's in a greenhouse. It has a lot of space left to grow before it hits the glass roof.'

Mrs Wahid sighed. 'I really have to go back to the Botanic Garden sometime soon. It has been quite a while since I have been there.' She rubbed her knees. 'I am sorry not to be getting up today. The rain is making my old bones ache. Be grateful for your young legs! You will miss them one day!'

Caspia looked down at her legs. Her jeans were wet and dirty from kneeling on the sidewalk. But Mrs. Wahid did not seem to be bothered by this at all.

'So...' She leaned back in her chair with an expectant smile. 'Tell me, which kind of cinnamon was your favorite!'

'The sticks. Definitely,' said Caspia. 'Mom thought so too. She made a delicious mushroom ragout with them.'

'Mushroom ragout!' Mrs Wahid raised her eyebrows

in delight. 'You'll have to give me the recipe. My fingers are always impatient when baking or cooking and I am constantly burning them, but I love trying out new recipes!' She rubbed her ringed fingers as if they remembered too many hot pans.

'What about dandelion? Is that also a spice, Mrs Wahid?'

The old woman laughed. 'Most people would probably call that one a weed. So many useful plants are dismissed as weeds. It is a shame! And evidence of human ignorance. Dandelion is a truly astonishing plant—healer, chef, adventurer! I would call it a wild herb. Is dandelion the answer to another riddle?'

Caspia nodded. 'I found two and collected some of their seeds...'

'... And now you need soil!' Mrs Wahid pointed her bejeweled fingers toward the back of the store. 'There should be a bag in the courtyard in the back. I am growing some herbs there. Just the usual. Some parsley, chives, tarragon, nasturtium...'

Heavens! More names Caspia did not know. How many citizens did the Green Kingdom have? Monyet followed her on his short, crooked legs, as she walked toward the back door. But this time he didn't growl or bark.

Mrs Wahid's courtyard was barely larger than a beach

towel, but gorgeous old ceramic pots lined the edges. The plants inside them were a lush green and one of them was covered in bright orange flowers.

'You're all really beautiful,' Caspia said as she filled the aluminum can with soil from the plastic bag that was resting against the wall. 'And how good you smell! Unfortunately, I have no idea what you're called. Rosalind definitely would've known. She would only have had to run her fingers over your leaves!'

Monyet did not have much respect for the courtyard's green inhabitants. He raised a leg to pee against one of the pots and bared his tiny teeth when Caspia shooed him away. No, they would most likely never be friends. Most dogs could sense that she was scared of them, since a terrier had chased her into her grandparents' garden shed on her seventh birthday.

Monyet disappeared underneath Mrs Wahid's chair again after following Caspia back into the store. But she could see that he was watching her.

'Ah, good, you found it.' Mrs Wahid gave her a satisfied nod. 'Put a glass over the can after you plant the seeds. That will help them sprout more quickly. Cover the seeds in only a small amount of soil and keep it moist, but not too moist. Take away the glass once you see the little plants.'

Apparently, it was quite complicated setting up a nursery for little dandelion plants!

Mom was still at one of her cooking classes when Caspia got back to the apartment. So far Mom had really enjoyed them. She had even come to think that the people in Brooklyn were friendlier than those in Wilmerton. Caspia had definitely never met anyone like Mrs Wahid before. Or someone like Margaret from the Botanic Garden.

The four dandelion seeds looked so tiny when Caspia fished them out of her wallet that it seemed a little silly to believe they would turn into fully grown plants. Caspia expected that Laryssa and Ellie would say the same thing when she sent them pictures of the tiny seeds inside the aluminum can. But they were fascinated by it all, especially by Mrs Wahid's instructions. And when Caspia looked at her little glass-aluminum greenhouse, she had to admit that it looked really nice on the windowsill—especially after Ellie suggested that she wrap the can in one of the colorful paper napkins that Mom liked to buy.

On the second drawer of the dresser bloomed a dandelion. So yes, Minna had of course solved this riddle as well. What might her embroidered dandelion portrait have looked like? Probably like the embroidered pillows in the living room.

Caspia very much admired what Minna could paint using needle and thread. But the work on her windowsill garden was more to her liking. Her teacher Mrs Pokorny had tried for years to teach her how to sew, to no avail. The needle inevitably found its way into her finger. For a while, Ellie had called her Sleeping Beauty because of this. Ellie did not have much of a gift for sewing either. But Laryssa was very skilled with her hands in general. She could patch and sew her own dresses and even fixed her little brother's remote-controlled toys. 'I just like to understand how things work,' she had explained after taking no time at all to repair the toaster that had already stumped Caspia's dad.

Have you ever done any embroidery, Laryssa? Caspia texted while heating up the food that Mom had left on the stove for her. A flood of photos was her response: the torn knee of Laryssa's favorite jeans, patched up with embroidered hearts. Coffee stains on a T-shirt, covered up with embroidered birds. And a bag that had a decorative pattern made of her initials. Why had she never told them that she could do embroidery? **Because embroidery is such an old lady thing!** was Laryssa's response.

Despite all this she didn't want to embroider a dandelion.

When Caspia told her mother about the dandelion that

weathered shoes and bicycle tires, Mom tried to convince her to pick a few leaves so she could cook something with them. But Caspia explained that the Brooklyn dandelion needed all of its strength to survive in this place, and that she would definitely not pluck off its leaves and further reduce its chances at survival. In response to which Mom announced that she would find another way to serve them a dandelion dish.

And she did.

She actually managed to find fresh dandelion leaves in a shop and made the most delicious dandelion eggs with them.

Rosalind's Third Letter

June 23, 1958

Hello Minna!

I think your dandelion was the best thing you have embroidered so far! I could feel all the seeds underneath their parachutes, and the jagged leaves bit my fingers. Bravo! Every blind girl should have a sister who likes to embroider.

You solved my first two riddles so effortlessly! I hope you will not be disappointed that this one will probably be even easier. It is difficult to find a clue that does not immediately give away the identity of this duchess of the Green Kingdom. But Papa was also of the opinion that our game would not be complete without her. Especially after we have just been to a French garden that was dedicated entirely to her.

So...

1. She always wears armor and kills princes.

2. The Indian god Vishnu created his bride Lakshmi from her petals.

3. When her petals are red, the blood of a nightingale is said to be responsible.

4. Some say she is a nymph who was turned into a flower by a god.

5. In England they named a war after her.

I am sure you already know who this riddle is about.
I can't wait to see how you will make her bloom.
There are humble and noble members of her family!

Enchant my senses, sister, with a plant that many call a queen.

With love that has traveled to you all the way from France!
Your Rosalind

Blooms and Books

Rosalind had been right. The third riddle was indeed the easiest so far. There was only one plant, as far as Caspia knew, that killed princes. But just to be sure, she checked online whether the same flower had given its petals for Lakshmi. Yes, it was the same. The fourth clue also fit: it was indeed said that it had been a nymph once.

Ellie researched the story with the nightingale and Laryssa knew everything about the war that was named after the flower, because it had inspired her favorite TV show. One detail that Rosalind had not mentioned, however: that the plant was also hidden in her name.

Rosa. The rose.

Mom was thrilled by this new challenge because, as

she announced over breakfast, the petals of roses made for wonderful decorations. Mom had decided to come up with a new recipe for every plant that Caspia investigated. And even Dad had started to ask where his daughter's sudden new interest in plants came from. Caspia really hated lying to the two of them, but she was still worried that her parents would give the letters to the landlady and she would never get the chance to solve the rest of Rosalind's riddles. So she stuck to the story that somebody was posting plant riddles online, and Dad did not ask any further questions because there were a thousand decisions to make at the construction site.

Caspia had to admit that it was also fun to have a secret that she only shared with her two best friends—and Mrs Wahid.

Rose. That's easy. You just have to find a flower shop, Laryssa texted. They all decided to read *Sleeping Beauty* again, to remind themselves of the dangers that this flower brought. And Ellie sent a picture of a tattoo with a fairy in a rose blossom and announced that she would get this as soon as she turned eighteen. To which Laryssa responded that Ellie wouldn't dare get a tattoo for her eighteenth birthday because Ellie was, as they all knew, afraid of needles.

A flower shop. Yes.

Dad had already been up on his scaffolding for hours and Mom was at a cooking class that promised to introduce her to the secrets of Moroccan cuisine. So Caspia decided to head out in search of roses.

The flower shop that sounded the most interesting was barely a five-minute walk away and very close to Mrs Wahid's store.

Blooms & Books.

That was a rather unusual name, Caspia thought. And yes, right in the window, Caspia spotted a vase of roses. And a silver music stand holding a book with a rose on its cover.

The shop's front door had been propped open, welcoming her inside—as if the owner believed that the flowers still liked to feel the fresh air, even though they had lost their roots. The scents that greeted her when she stepped through the door were very different from those in Mrs Wahid's store. They were much sweeter, like somebody had mixed together a dozen different perfumes. When Caspia closed her eyes, it was immediately much easier to pick them apart: strong and shy scents, dark and light, loud and quiet. Which one came from the roses? Rosalind surely could have told her.

'You're the first person to walk in here and close her eyes,' she heard a voice say. 'Usually our customers like the way I decorate.'

Caspia hastily opened her eyes. 'Oh, I like it, too. I was just trying to smell all the scents.'

'Ah, I see, I'll have to try that some time!' The girl behind the counter closed her eyes. She was only a few years older than Caspia, maybe sixteen or seventeen. 'Hmmm, I know what you mean. You can tell more easily how different they all are. I should do that more often.'

She was rather tall and her skin was almost as dark as her hair, which was speckled with tiny yellow flowers that seemed to sprout right from the thick dark curls.

'Is this a book AND flower shop?' Caspia asked.

The question sounded a bit silly, but she had never seen a store like this. The wall to her right and half of the back wall were covered in bookshelves. There were books on stands between the vases. And pillars painted with books, with flower pots on top. Bookmarks dangled off the plants that were creeping out of baskets underneath the ceiling. And between the vases and pots that were arranged all over the floor, Caspia discovered a few figures that were clearly from famous novels. Yes, right there, that was Winnie-the-Pooh. He was sitting in front of a honey jar. And one of the Wild Things was shimmying up that pot over there.

'No, it is really just a flower shop.' The girl carried a vase to the window and placed it between the others.

'It's my aunt's,' she said as she took a step back to study the effect. 'She believes that flowers tell stories. We don't always agree but on that point we do. It's not easy keeping the water away from the books, especially those in the window. But flowers and books look so nice together, don't they?'

Caspia nodded. Blooms & Books was the most beautiful flower shop she had ever seen. As well as the most beautiful bookstore. If it had been one.

'What are the books about?'

'Plants. You wouldn't believe how many stories there are about them. Stories about enchanted flowers and magic trees... My aunt has been collecting them her whole life. She has so many by now that she doesn't have the space to keep them all at home anymore. That's why she started to bring them here! But the books aren't for sale...even though a lot of people ask about them!'

She let her eyes roam across the shelves.

'Some of the stories are pretty strange,' she sighed. 'Like the fairytale about the juniper tree. So creepy! I like the Greek myths. All the nymphs that turn into flowers...'

Hadn't that been one of Rosalind's clues for the rose?

'Jemila!' a voice rang out through the curtain behind the store counter. 'Stop chatting. Sell flowers. That's why we're here.'

Jemila made a face. 'My aunt isn't feeling well,' she whispered. 'That's why I'm taking care of everything today. Usually she's happy with how I run the shop. But yesterday a woman came by to buy an expensive orchid, and I couldn't stop myself from saying that I think orchids are boring. They ARE boring! Don't you think? They have about as much scent as a plastic bottle!'

Caspia eyed the orchids on the counter. Her grandma loved them, but Caspia had to agree with Jemila.

'I always think that their leaves and flowers feel like somebody made them out of wax,' she whispered.

Jemila gave her a conspiratorial smile.

'Don't worry. She doesn't want to buy an orchid, Zia!' she called. 'She is here to...' She looked at Caspia and raised a questioning eyebrow.

'A rose. I'm here to buy a rose,' she said out loud.

'Just one?' came the retort from the back. 'We only sell roses in bouquets.'

Jemila rolled her eyes and winked at Caspia.

'What kind of rose are you looking for?' She pointed toward the window with a sweeping gesture. 'We have queens, witches, wild girls, ballroom beauties... I think roses are like people. They play many different parts and dress for every occasion.'

Caspia liked the way that Jemila talked about flowers. Rosalind surely would have felt the same way. *What kind of rose are you looking for?* There were a few gorgeous, long-stemmed roses with deep red blossoms in a tall black porcelain vase. But she also liked the bouquet in the clay jug next to it. It consisted of much smaller roses that opened their flat white blossoms between finely toothed leaves. The flower petals made Caspia think of feathers, they were so light and playful on the thorny stems.

Jemila of course noticed which vases caught her eye.

'That one,' she pointed to the dark red roses, 'is the empress. At least that's what I call her.'

She pointed toward the bookshelves. 'There are many tales about roses such as these. She has been bred and cultivated for so long that she's forgotten her own origin and believes that she has nothing in common with the wild roses that are her ancestors. The empress is convinced that you need a greenhouse to grow proper buds, as well as a lot of artificial fertilizer. These roses on the other hand...' Jemila walked over to the clay jug, '...still remember the meadows and hedges and how much fun it was to climb up trees. They produce absolutely delicious rose hips. You can make beautiful wreaths from them, and...' she carefully pulled one from the jug, '...these roses have a wonderful scent!'

She held it out to Caspia, gesturing for her to take it. The thorny stem was much thinner than that of the empress, and it had many small branches. Caspia sniffed one of the white blossoms. Oh yes. She could immediately see a wild meadow in the forest, with bees and butterflies swarming around.

'This is *Rosa canina*,' Jemila explained. 'She is a wild rose. That is to say, she was not bred by humans. My aunt doesn't like her,' she whispered to Caspia, 'because she loses her petals much faster and more easily than the empress! That makes her harder to sell. But I believe that the really old fairy tales mean this one when they mention roses.'

She put the small rose back in with the others, emanating their heady scent, and pulled out a long-stemmed empress from the porcelain vase. 'Her floral highness will last for many days when fed right. But…'

Jemila held the dark red blossom out under Caspia's nose.

'She doesn't have any scent at all!'

Jemila shrugged her shoulders and put the rose back with her sisters. 'Nobody is perfect. Although the empress does a very good job at pretending she is.'

Yes, that she did. And Caspia took a picture of her even though she didn't have a scent. And one of the wild roses. Then she let her gaze wander over the other vases. Too many choices! And she couldn't afford to bring more than one of them home. Flowers, as Blooms & Books had taught her, were pretty expensive. Which made sense when you considered how much work it was to raise them, and pick them, let alone getting them all into flower shops.

'I'll take this one.' Caspia pointed toward the clay jug.

Jemila seemed very happy with her choice.

'I'll give you three!' she whispered. 'For the price of one.'

Caspia tried to protest. The aunt in the backroom sounded very severe. But Jemila only put her finger to her lips.

'Two dollars,' she said out loud, as she wrapped the three roses in pink tissue paper. 'Be careful when you unwrap them,' she added in a quiet voice. 'My aunt is right. They really do lose their petals very easily.'

She handed Caspia the bouquet. '*Rosa canina* means dog rose. It is said that her roots can heal bite wounds caused by a rabid dog. But I've also read that it's because her petals look like a dog's teeth.'

Caspia handed Jemila the two dollars. 'Have you read all the books here?'

'That'll take me a few more years, I think. And not all of them are very good!'

They definitely looked inviting. Many of their spines were covered in bright colors or elaborate patterns. And their wooden shelves were decorated with carved flowers, fruits, and vines. There was even a worn-out green armchair in front of the back shelf that whispered: *sit down and read!*

'My friend Ellie would be so happy in this shop. She'd lose her mind!' Caspia said. 'And my friend Laryssa would love the empress.'

Laryssa was a little bit like the empress, Caspia thought. Proud, a bit touchy, and occasionally rather thorny. Ellie, on the other hand, had more in common with the dog rose: playful, with a sweet scent and an abundance of flowers, which she would happily lose in exchange for red rose hips.

'Can I take a picture of the store?' Caspia asked. 'For my friends?'

'No!' called the voice behind the curtain. 'No photos!'

'Yeah, yeah, all right, Zia!' Jemila called back, giving Caspia a sign to take the picture anyway.

'She's only worried about the regulations,' she whispered. 'You're not really allowed to have this many books in a flower shop.'

That was a shame. It was so wonderful.

Caspia walked along one of the shelves and ran her finger along the spines. '*Plants: Songs and Legends*,' she read. '*Flower Myths*, *The Cabaret of Plants*, *Roses and Stories*...'

Jemila walked up next to her and pulled a book off the

shelf. 'You might like this one. And maybe this one too.' She pulled out a second one. 'This one is about weeds! It's way more exciting than it sounds. And the other one might not look very promising, but it has the strangest stories!'

'Can I lend her a book, Zia?' she called in the direction of the curtain. 'Or two.'

It was quiet for a moment. 'Oh well, why not. But she has to give you her address. And return the books next week.'

'Don't be deceived! She's glad when someone actually reads them,' Jemila whispered, as she put the two books in Caspia's basket. 'Like me, she thinks that books get terribly bored when they sit on shelves.'

That was probably true, even though Caspia had never thought about books in that way.

'Thanks!' she said. 'Do you know stories about all the flowers you sell?'

'No, only those I really like. But...' Jemila laughed, '... I like most of them! I want to have my own plant nursery one day! Somewhere in the country. And my flowers will smell amazing AND be beautiful, and they will tell a thousand stories about all the different places they come from.'

'Maybe you can open one in Maine,' Caspia said. 'There's a lot of land there. But it can also get terribly cold.'

'That could be a problem!' Jemila shuddered. 'Many

plants like the sun as much as I do!'

She lowered her voice once more. 'My Zia always says these are peculiar ideas, but really she likes them. She's taught me much about plants. And this shop...' she added in a loud voice, '...is a bit peculiar as well when you think about it!!!'

Caspia thought she could hear laughter behind the curtain.

'Here. A little something extra.' Jemila took a small sachet of seeds from a basket on the counter and handed it to Caspia. 'Nasturtium. You can eat the flowers. Same with roses, did you know that? Just make sure they haven't been treated with insecticides. Most flowers have tons of them on their petals.' She sighed. 'Because they raise them like armies! All in neat rows and all the same. Flowers like to mingle with others! They don't want to stand around with their own kind. Because that's boring! And unhealthy! That's true of people as well, don't you think?'

'Jemila!' came the voice from the room in the back. 'Are you still talking out there?'

'Only to myself,' Jemila called back.

She winked at Caspia and waved goodbye. When Caspia stopped in front of the window outside, Jemila was sitting in the green armchair, reading.

Flowers to Eat

Mom found a blue vase in one of the kitchen cabinets that was perfect for Caspia's dog roses. The simple white blossoms looked as delicate as butterflies that had landed between the leaves. Caspia decided to convince her grandmother to plant dog roses in her garden. She had more than enough empresses.

Mom loved the dog roses as well, but she was even more thrilled about Jemila's seed gift.

'Nasturtium,' she cried out. 'These flowers turn every salad into a fairytale. They're red and orange and yellow and taste sooo peppery! How fast do they grow?'

Caspia looked at the small sachet. 'It says here it'll take four weeks. But you won't be able to pick them and cook with them yet!'

Mom looked very disappointed. 'I heard that you can also eat the petals of roses,' she said.

Caspia gave her a strict look. 'My dog roses are not for cooking!'

She made Mom swear on her spice jars that she wouldn't touch them. Caspia wondered if Jemila's aunt had a book about edible plants, and decided to ask Jemila about it next time.

They found a dark green bowl with a white floral pattern for the seeds. The upper edge was a little worn and it looked like it was made for raising plant children. Maybe Minna had used it in the same way back in the day? There was just enough of Mrs Wahid's soil left to fill the bowl. The nasturtium seeds did not seem to have anything at all in common with the seeds she had picked off the brave dandelion. They were definitely too heavy to travel the world by parachute!

'Rosalind! Minna!' Caspia said, setting the bowl down on her windowsill. 'What do you think? Do you like my garden?'

For a moment she believed she could see a girl smile

between the flowers on the wallpaper. Although...were ghosts the same age as when they died, or did they grow young again? Ellie liked this question. **Maybe you can choose**, she wrote back. **At least I hope so.**

Laryssa did not believe in ghosts. She also did not believe that Ellie's cat Boomer was a reincarnation of Ellie's great-aunt Ingrid. Caspia did believe that! Because Boomer scratched her every time she tried to sit in the old rocking chair where Ingrid had liked to sit.

Ellie had almost packed her bags to come to Brooklyn when Caspia sent the pictures she had taken in Blooms & Books.

She sent a thousand questions—about the flowers, the books, and about Jemila. Laryssa wanted to know what kind of flowers had been in her hair because she wanted to try to copy the look. And she asked if there had been any change in the dandelion babies.

Caspia proudly sent her a picture of the four tiny plants that were now growing in the aluminum can. She had watched a time-lapse video to find out how long it would take until they became real flowers. At least two months. But they would blossom while they were still in Brooklyn—if nothing got in the way. Ellie and Laryssa were already hoping that Caspia would bring seeds from her dandelion back to Maine. But she would have to move them to a real flowerpot soon. It was already getting a little tight in the can and Ellie had informed her that she should have drilled a hole in the bottom of the can so that any extra water could drain away. The two of them acted as if they had invented gardening! Laryssa had even sent her a tutorial that explained how you potted plants correctly. Well, the green bowl didn't have a hole in the bottom either and therefore was not ideal for the nasturtium. Caspia had seen beautiful clay pots at Blooms & Books. But they had been pretty expensive.

Mom called her for dinner and served a delicious-smelling dish to Moroccan music that she had prepared in a tagine—a strangely shaped ceramic dish that Dad almost broke when he tried to take a closer look. They all ate so much, Dad swore he wouldn't be able to get another bite down for at least three days and suggested an evening walk. Mom went with him, but Caspia decided that she was taking enough walks during her plant excursions. She would get cozy in bed with Jemila's books instead. Laryssa sent a video in which she tried to put a red rose into her pale-blonde hair without success, and finally ate one of its petals in frustration, which was a little strange. Ellie had found a Romanian fairytale in which a man was born from a rosebud. And Caspia read in one of the books that the rose was dedicated to the goddess Venus. It turned into a very cozy evening, and the dog rose made it even nicer.

Rosalind's Fourth Letter

April 10, 1959

Oh Minna!

The rose portrait is so good that I sniff my fingers every time I touch it. And indeed! They always smell like roses. Did you put a little rose oil onto the thread to enchant your little sister?

Ah, is our game not the most wonderful fun? Almost as if you were here with us.

Here comes the fourth of your green riddles:

1. She is as strong as steel although she weighs much less.

2. She is a great musician and said to have grown from the sixth finger of a goddess.

3. She is the fastest-growing plant in the world.

4. She does not only make disinfecting bandages. You can also cook delicious food with her.

5. There is an animal that cannot live without this plant.

Hmmm, this last clue probably made it too easy again!

Papa and I are in China at the moment. The people here believe that ghosts live in the plant that you have to guess this time—and that the first man and the first woman were made from its stalks.

Oh no, Rosalind, now you have really made it too easy! I am sorry, Minna! I am so enchanted by this plant. Perhaps this time, instead of embroidery, you can send me a flute that was carved from it as proof that you have solved the riddle.

I send a hug that is as firm and strong
as my mystery plant!
Your Rosalind

The Boy

Yes, the fifth clue made it easy! But Laryssa, Ellie, and Caspia all agreed that the clue with the finger was the most fascinating. Caspia found the story about it in one of Jemila's books: the goddess that Rosalind had written about was Sita, the wife of the Indian god Rama (who was actually an incarnation of the god Vishnu—Hindu deities were endlessly fascinating but also confusing). Sita had a sixth finger on her hand that she broke off and planted so that it grew into—of course—bamboo!

Bambusa vulgaris. Caspia liked the botanical name a lot.

Caspia's internet research revealed that bamboo grew up to twenty-four inches a day. That confirmed the third clue. And regarding the fourth: yes, bandages made from bamboo were very good because only harmless bacteria could live on it. Clue number five caused Ellie to flood their chat with cute panda photos. But she also sent an article about how deforestation endangered bamboo and therefore also the pandas. Ellie had enlisted her and Laryssa many times to fish plastic out of the river or to support protests against illegal fishing methods with at least their signatures. Caspia had to admit that until now she had mostly found Ellie's enthusiasm a little over the top. But the four delicate little plants on her windowsill were convincing proof that Ellie was right. The Green Kingdom was in danger and they all had to become its protectors! Had this danger already been so pressing when Rosalind had written the letters? No, probably not. Caspia frowned as she looked at Ellie's panda photos. Maybe she should also join the Wilmerton Greenlings when she was back home...

Laryssa found out that bamboo was called *Zhu* in Chinese, and sent a photo of the bamboo stalks that her mother used to hold up her tomatoes. But what exactly did the living plant look like? The internet gave her the answer of course. But—Rosalind surely would have asked—how did it smell and feel?

Caspia decided that it was time for another visit to the Botanic Garden. Mom was at her latest cooking class:

Indian dishes that Western tongues can survive. And Dad had moved up another level on his scaffolding. Just the thought made Caspia dizzy. Especially when he sent pictures of his coffee cup with the Manhattan skyline or Jamaica Bay in the background.

According to the Botanic Garden's website, there were bamboo plants of the 'yellow groove' variety at the stairs between the desert and the tropical pavilions.

I see you guys have nice weather. You should bring a picnic, Laryssa suggested.

Unfortunately, that was not allowed at the Botanic Garden. Caspia had noticed the signs during her last visit. It was a real shame though. There were so many tempting picnic spots. The Bluebell Wood, the Fragrance Garden, or the one for Native Flora! But she didn't have to have a proper picnic. Surely no one would mind if she had a bite to eat or a sip of tea somewhere? So she packed some Tupperware with Mom's Moroccan food and filled a thermos with the cardamom tea they had drunk with it. Cardamom: a spice made from the seeds of a plant. That had been the vague information on Wikipedia. Mrs Wahid would definitely be able to tell her more.

It was a wonderfully warm summer day, the kind that was all too rare in Wilmerton. The sky above the street was a river of blue, and Caspia walked past a Chinese restaurant whose menu sported many bamboo dishes. Braised spring bamboo shoots, mushrooms and bamboo shoots, steamed bamboo shoots with soy sauce...the restaurant was still closed but maybe she could convince her parents to eat here sometime? Even though Mom could be very critical at restaurants—which was really embarrassing at times.

Caspia was thrilled when Margaret recognized her right away, and the bamboo that grew between the two pavilions was hard to miss, with its unmistakable stalks and all those long, slender leaves. When Caspia closed her eyes, her fingertips found a stalk that was almost as smooth as porcelain, and the leaves really did run across her skin with the featherlight touch of a ghost. It was not difficult to imagine that the very first man and woman had been made from bamboo.

'You can buy little bamboo plants in the Garden's shop over there. They grow very fast.'

Caspia hastily opened her eyes.

A boy was smiling at her. The boy she had accidentally taken a photo of when she came to see the cinnamon tree. He was a little bit taller than her and probably around her age, with short black hair and eyes that were almost as dark as Jemila's.

'Hi,' he said. 'I am Ado. I think I have seen you here once before. In the tropical pavilion.'

Heavens, was she blushing? That would never have happened to Laryssa. And Ellie only blushed with girls anyway.

'Hi. Caspia...nice to meet you.' She actually managed not to sound too nervous. Or did she? 'Do you come here often?'

The bamboo brushed its leaves across her arm like a green friend. *I took a photo of you,* she almost added. *But not on purpose.*

'Yeah, pretty often,' Ado said. 'My father works here.'

He pointed to the bamboo. 'Why did you close your eyes when you touched the leaves?'

Because I found the letters of a girl who was blind and traveled the world to meet plants. No. That story was too strange and complicated to tell a boy she had only seen once before through the branches of a cinnamon tree. And who made her blush.

'Oh, I... I just like getting to know plants with my fingers,' she mumbled instead. That sounded completely bizarre but Ado seemed to like that answer.

'I feel the same way,' he said. 'I use my fingers and a pencil.'

Yes, I know! Caspia wanted to say. *And I would really like to see your sketches.* But was that too forward? 'You think too much when it comes to boys,' Laryssa had once told her. Well, she generally just liked to think about things. Although she had to admit that it could be a bit annoying sometimes. 'But she's only twelve,' she had heard Dad say the first time she had a crush on a boy and Mom had pointed it out to him. Yes, that could happen even at twelve. The very first time she'd had that strange fluttery feeling in her heart and stomach she had actually only been eight. Ben Travers. She had been sure that she would marry him. She had even planned the wedding. On a boat on the river.

'It's so nice here,' she said. 'It is a shame you're not allowed to have picnics, isn't it?'

Well done, she could hear Laryssa whisper.

'Oh, it's all right. You just have to find a quiet spot,' Ado said. 'And not put down a blanket on the grass because that causes bare spots.'

He smiled at her. 'I'm actually on my way to draw wild geese. They love the water garden here!'

He waved at her one last time and strolled off.

Can I watch when you draw the geese? Laryssa would have called after him. *I have Moroccan food and cardamom tea!* But Caspia could not say that sort of thing to someone she had only just met for the first time. Even if she liked that someone as much as Ado. Yes, she really liked him, even though they had only exchanged a few sentences.

Ping. A text message from Laryssa. As if she had smelled it. **What are you doing right now? Have you found the bamboo?**

Yes, Caspia replied. She sent her and Ellie a photo, but this time without Ado in the background. She would tell them about him later.

Ado was right: Caspia spotted several visitors who had brought a thermos and a small snack. In the rose garden there were many empresses but she did not spot any *Rosa canina*. The garden for native plants was buzzing and humming with bees and other insects. And Caspia decided that this was exactly the right spot to have a sip of Mom's tea. The grass was tall and wild here and the flowers did not grow in neatly separated beds. She liked that very much.

A sign explained that in many gardens there were no bees or butterflies, because the garden centers where people bought their plants mostly sold trees, bushes, and flowers from faraway countries, and native insects did not know what to do with them. The blossoms that surrounded Caspia were fairly inconspicuous compared with the ones she had seen in the flowerbeds here so far. But all the swarming life proved that the humble flowers were apparently much more important for the Green Kingdom than the empresses. Caspia took pictures of the signs with their names: Big Bluestem Grass, Butterfly Weed, Sheep Laurel, and—her favorite name—*Pyxidanthera barbulata*. Then she settled down on the grass and poured herself some of Mom's tea.

All right, she had to admit: it really was an adventure to be in a new place, even though Brooklyn was not as far away from Maine as the Amazon. A different Caspia emerged here. A Brooklyn-Caspia, just like the Brooklyn-dandelion. Did all places do that? If so, should people move places regularly? To meet all their different selves? *Well, Caspia*, she thought, taking a sip of the delicious tea. *It's probably best not to voice that thought out loud. Or your parents might like the idea. And then what?*

No, it was good to be at home in one place. Wasn't it?

Besides...wasn't the only reason she liked Brooklyn so much because Rosalind's letters had taught her to discover the Green Kingdom between all the houses and streets?

She got up and picked a few pieces of grass off her clothes. For a moment she was tempted to take them with her and plant them in her windowsill garden. But it was probably too small for a wild meadow. She turned her face up to the sun and closed her eyes.

Two more days before she would open the next letter. She had almost packed one to open here. But Caspia was glad she hadn't done that. This day was perfect just as it was.

Rosalind's Fifth Letter

June 21, 1959

Dear Minna,

The bamboo flute you sent arrived safely at our hotel in Kashgar. And every time I blow into it, it sings of China—and of the sixth finger of an Indian goddess.

Thank you very, very much! Papa also plays it sometimes. I think he misses you very much. But like me, he is glad that you are so happy living in Brooklyn where you embroider ballgowns and theater costumes! Next year I will come to visit you and admire them! Promise!

The plant you are meant to guess today, you have definitely —

No, I have to stop always giving everything away too soon! Here are the clues:

1. It comes from the mountains of Kazakhstan.

2. Its fruit plays a dangerous part in several famous stories.

3. There are over 7,500 varieties of this plant.

4. When you dream about it, it promises wealth, beauty, and happiness—although I am not sure in what order.

5. The Celts buried their dead with the fruit of this plant to ensure their rebirth. The Norse gods even owe their immortality to it.

Papa suggests that you send us some of its seeds once you have guessed this particular citizen of the Green Kingdom. He wants to plant them at the feet of the angel by Mama's grave, the one he brought back from Italy. He says the seeds are known for producing offspring that are very different from the parent plant, but Mama would like that. Papa and I will be back in Scotland for the seventh anniversary of her death. We will bring her roses from our garden and a piece of her favorite cake (chocolate with cherries) like every year. But this time Papa will also read her all the riddles we have sent you so far. And we will tell Mama how happy you are in Brooklyn! That will make her happy, too.

Much love from Kashgar!
Your Rosalind

At the Feet of an Angel

Its fruit plays a dangerous part in several famous stories. Caspia was embarrassed to admit how long it took her to work out what plant Rosalind's fifth riddle was about despite this clue. Maybe she had been too distracted by the mention of her mother's grave. Rosalind must have been a little girl when she died, and Minna might have been Caspia's age.

Maybe Laryssa was the first to solve the riddle because the passage did not move her in the same way. She didn't have an easy relationship with her mother, and Caspia knew that she often envied her and Ellie theirs.

Apple! The answer is most definitely apple, Laryssa wrote. **But where the devil is Kazakhstan?**

Of course, it was apple! Although Caspia never knew that the Norse gods had to eat apples to be immortal.

Ellie sent a map on which she had not only marked Kazakhstan but also Scotland. **Isn't it nice that she brings cake to her mother's grave?** she wrote. **We should start doing that for my brother. Chocolate cake! He always requested it!** Ellie's older brother had died of cancer two years ago.

Mom was in the kitchen, cursing as she retrieved something rather burnt-looking from the oven.

'I've told your father a thousand times not to call me when I'm baking or cooking!' she yelled.

Which was not easy given that she was almost always doing either one or the other. Caspia gave her a hug. A very tight one.

'What's going on?' Mom asked, scrutinizing her face. 'Are you feeling a little homesick? Should I maybe make you the mushroom ragout again, the one that smells like cinnamon and adventure?'

'No, no,' Caspia replied. 'It's all good. It's just...don't die, okay?'

She still hadn't told her parents about the letters. Right now she regretted that.

'I promise you that I'll try not to,' Mom said. 'Do I look pale or sickly? I swear that's only from my failed bamboo recipe!'

Mom had been very impressed with the restaurant that Caspia had discovered on her way to the Botanic Garden, and she liked the bamboo dishes so much that she had tried to make them herself. But so far she had been very disappointed with the results. By now she was so dejected that she had described herself as a mediocre amateur cook and agreed with Grandma that her cookbook was a ridiculous pipedream.

'Why don't you make something with apples instead, Mom?' Caspia suggested. 'How about...apple soup, maybe?'

A friend of Mom's always made that. She had a huge old apple tree in her backyard. When Caspia was small, she had picked the apple blossoms off her clothes and hair and had made her own version of that soup for her stuffed animals. She had climbed around that tree so often that her fingers knew its leaves, bark, flowers, and fruit like the back of her hand. So, she decided not to go on the hunt for another tree in Brooklyn, but to go buy some apples at the corner grocer instead. She would save the seeds and take them home, and then she would plant Brooklyn apple trees in Wilmerton with Ellie and Laryssa. Yes, that sounded like a good plan.

Mom liked the idea of apple soup à la Brooklyn. 'Yes, with olive oil and thyme,' she murmured. 'And pumpkin!'

But she could be very stubborn when her cooking didn't turn out the way she wanted it to, and she couldn't give up on bamboo quite yet. When she started listening to punk music from the seventies in the kitchen (always a sign that she was VERY disgruntled), Caspia decided to visit Blooms & Books. She bought some apples at the grocer on her way there. They were very red. And looked creepily perfect.

'Like Snow White's apple,' Jemila decided when Caspia set them down on the counter. They were luckily not poisoned but they tasted a bit like plastic. They quickly found three different stories about apples in Jemila's aunt's books, while they dispelled the plastic taste in their mouths with cookies that Jemila seemed to magically summon from some drawer in the counter. Occasionally customers came into the store, and Caspia was very impressed with how quickly Jemila assembled and wrapped up the most beautiful bouquets for them. Her Zia was visiting a friend, and no voice came from behind the curtain. So Caspia finally introduced Jemila to her friends in Maine, and in return Jemila introduced her to the art of flower-arranging. After that they replaced the orchid on the shop's counter with a vase of dog roses next to which they put a spectacularly cheesy-looking book of fairytales. Caspia wanted to return the orchid to the counter before she left, but Jemila was sure that her aunt would like the new set-up. And she was right. The next day she posted a thumbs up into the group chat that Ellie had started for all of them—and a picture that showed the shop's counter that still featured the dog roses and the fairytale book.

When Caspia got back to the apartment (hooray, the elevator finally worked!), Mom was still listening to punk music, battling with bamboo, and Dad had fallen asleep on the couch. The weather had been so hot recently that work at the construction site had been starting extra early. Caspia found his thermos cup filled with water and a dusty flower on her bedside table. *I found this at the construction site*, read a note in Dad's messy handwriting that was tucked underneath the thermos. *I am sure it will have a much nicer time in your windowsill garden.*

It was a thistle. It stung Caspia's fingers when she carefully wiped the dust off its leaves and flowers, but it looked fantastic. Ellie identified it as a plume thistle, which was apparently very popular with insects that were important for the pollination of all sorts of plants. It was fascinating how many of those creatures there were! Ellie had developed a passion for wild bees recently and had told her that there were even green bees out there.

At breakfast the next morning, Mom announced that bamboo had turned out to be an unvanquishable foe. Then she ventured out to a class with the promising title *Witch Recipes from the Middle Ages*. Outside, the sun almost melted the tarmac, and Caspia decided that this was definitely a day for the Botanic Garden and Rosalind's sixth letter, even though she had really meant to wait one more day.

She packed a thermos with the leftover apple soup—yes, Mom had made a very interesting version à la Brooklyn!—and Rosalind's letter. Then she made her way to the headquarters of the Green Kingdom, as Ellie had christened the Brooklyn Botanic Garden.

Margaret was as nice as always, and Caspia decided to pay the Japanese Garden a visit this time around. She sat down near the koi pond, spooned the soup from the lid of her thermos—it was really delicious!—and opened the next pale-green envelope.

Apple blossom

Rosalind's Sixth Letter

September 12, 1959

Dearest Sister,

The apple seeds are sprouting at the feet of the angel guarding Mama. And Papa wears the tie you embroidered with apple blossoms every single Friday. And my fingers, which are generally quite clever, once again cannot fathom what your hands can create using a needle and thread! We both have very skillful hands, Minna! 'You got those from your mother, Rosa!' Papa likes to say. 'I cannot even pour a cup of tea without soaking the tablecloth!' That really does happen quite often.

All right... Back to our game! Today's riddle is about one of my favorite plants.

1. She too—like the rose—is said to have been a nymph once. But a jealous goddess turned her into a plant that grows so close to the ground that she gets trampled underfoot.

2. In the Middle Ages they used to strew it across the floor to keep away mice and fleas.

3. The oil contained in its leaves eases the breathing.

4. It can invade your whole garden with its sprawling arms if you do not keep it in check.

5. Some witches are said to make a brew from it that makes their enemies see double.

I hope this riddle is a little more difficult than the last one! Although Papa says that my third clue gives everything away again!

Watch out that you do not get turned into a plant by a goddess, Minna! Especially not into one that can get trampled. Even if a different god gifts you a healing scent as consolation.

All the best to Brooklyn from your sister,
Rosalind

Apple Soup and Tamales

Another nymph...sprawling arms...eases the breathing...a brew that makes you see double... Caspia looked up from Rosalind's letter and took another furtive sip of her apple soup. Which clue should she research first? She mostly had the Japanese Garden to herself now—except for a few sparrows who were very interested in her food. Was this one of the reasons why picnics were not allowed? To avoid a sparrow invasion?

'Is that a handwritten letter? I didn't even know those still existed!'

Ado stood a few steps away. Luckily her mind was still

so busy with Rosalind's riddle that she completely forgot to blush. *Thanks, Rosalind!*

'This one was written in 1959.' Caspia folded up the letter and put it back in the envelope. 'I think back then it was still pretty normal.'

She was really excited to see Ado. And he seemed to feel the same.

'Do you like apple soup?' She held out the thermos. 'My Mom made it. It's pretty amazing even though she thinks she's not a good cook right now.'

Heavens, why was she telling him that?

'Apple soup?' Ado sniffed at the thermos. 'I have never had apple soup! I can offer some tamales in exchange?' He sat down on the grass next to her.

Caspia filled the lid of the thermos with the rest of the soup and held out the spoon for him. After, despite Ado's protest, she had wiped it off with the edge of her T-shirt. In return, Ado handed her a paper bag. The content smelled so delicious that she was sure she was making a good trade, even though she did not know what tamales were exactly.

'Does this count as a picnic now?' she asked, slightly worried.

Ado looked around. 'I'd say no, we don't have a blanket with us, after all.'

He put a spoonful of the soup into his mouth and rolled his eyes in delight. 'Your mom is a fantastic cook. No matter what she thinks. What plant are you looking for today?'

He smiled when he saw how hesitantly Caspia was biting into the tamale's soft filling.

'Don't worry! It's just corn with some spices wrapped in a cornhusk. My mother never makes them differently. She is also a very good cook. Promise.'

Hmmmmmmm. That was delicious.

'Tamales,' she murmured. 'They taste as good as they sound.'

'I am glad.' Ado ate another spoonful of soup. 'So, why are you reading old letters?'

'I found them in a dresser. In the apartment we're renting for the summer.'

'Them?'

'There are ten. They each have a riddle about a plant.'

Never talk to boys about things that don't interest them, Laryssa had once told her. *Sports, cars, space exploration… those are all safe topics. Definitely not haircuts and fashion.* Ellie rolled her eyes whenever Laryssa gave tidbits of advice like that. She preferred the topic of space exploration over haircuts herself. Caspia suspected that Laryssa secretly did, too. Also… Ado surely did not mind talking about plants.

'The girl who wrote the letters was named Rosalind and she traveled the world with her botanist father. She wrote them to her sister, Minna. She was blind, that's why I close my eyes when I meet the plants she describes.'

'Was? Is she dead?'

'Well, the letters are over sixty years old!'

'So? My great-grandmother is ninety-six and determined to make it to a hundred.' Ado pointed toward Caspia's basket. 'Can I see the letter?'

Caspia was surprised that she didn't hesitate to pass him the envelope. Why did you trust some people right away and others not at all? Did plants trust other plants? Another question she would have liked to ask Rosalind.

Ado wiped his fingers clean on his jeans before he pulled Rosalind's letter from the envelope. Caspia liked that as well. She was still thinking about what Ado had said. Could it be that Rosalind was still alive? Minna was dead, but she had been the older sister.

'I think I know which plant she's talking about.' Ado looked up from the letter. 'Do you want me to tell you?'

Caspia shook her head fiercely. 'I have to work it out myself.'

'All right, no worries. I won't say anything. I swear.' Ado returned the letter to her with a smile. 'So bamboo was also one of these riddles? What were the others?'

'Cinnamon tree, dandelion, rose, and apple tree.'

'Interesting mix.' Ado reached into his backpack and pulled out a black notebook and a pencil. 'My father believes that plants watch us just as we watch them,' he said, as he started sketching the tree that was bent low over the koi pond. 'He says they talk to him. It might sound weird, but I believe him. Some plants might not say much, but I think grass, for example, is probably really chatty.'

Caspia had to laugh. Rosalind would have liked that theory.

Ado was bent low over his sketchbook, his hand moving swiftly and confidently over the pages. Caspia had told Ellie and Laryssa that she had met him again, though she didn't really know why. She just couldn't keep things like that to herself for long. Laryssa was now constantly asking for a new picture of him. Which was out of the question!

If only Ado hadn't looked so nice. She had to admit that she too would have liked to have another picture of him.

'Can I see your drawings?' she asked hesitantly.

'Sure.' Ado set the pencil down in the grass and handed her the sketchbook.

He tried to hide it, but he watched her as she turned the pages. It was the first time that Caspia noticed something like shyness in him. So she was not the only one, that was a relief!

'They're only sketches,' he said. 'Doodles. Nothing special.'

That wasn't true. Not at all. The sketches showed people, dogs, birds, and trees, sometimes done in black ink, sometimes in colored pencil, and they were all very, very good. Caspia turned another page. There was the sketch that Caspia had watched him work on through the branches of the cinnamon tree. Of the bush with the trumpet flowers.

'The flowers look exactly like this,' she said. 'You are so good, Ado!'

'No way.' He pretended to re-tie his shoelaces. 'They're only doodles.'

Doodles! Caspia closed the notebook just as carefully as Ado had put Rosalind's letter back in its envelope. 'Where did you learn to draw like that?'

Ado shrugged his shoulders. 'I've always liked to draw. My parents say ever since I was big enough to hold a pencil.'

He got up and wiped a few pieces of grass off his jeans. 'Sorry, I have to go. I promised my mother I'd pick up some groceries for her.'

He wrote something on the last page of his sketchbook and neatly tore out the piece of paper. 'Here. Text me when you're working on another plant riddle.'

He put the book back in his backpack and threw it over his shoulder.

'It starts with an M,' he called before walking back to the path that wound along the flower beds. The shadow that his narrow frame cast on the grass looked like it was dancing.

On her way home, Caspia caught herself smiling again and again. *It starts with an M.* Yes, she was pretty sure that she had solved Rosalind's riddle as well. Mint...it had to be mint. That clue that it eased the breathing had given Caspia the idea. She sat down on a bench and checked on her phone to see if there had been a nymph who had been turned into a plant that people trampled on. Yes. Minthe. There it was! And Persephone, the goddess of the underworld, had cursed poor Minthe because Hades, Persephone's husband, had liked her a little bit too much. He had tried to save her, and when he couldn't undo the curse, he gave her the most alluring scent, healing and fortifying at the same time.

Should she try to find a plant for her windowsill garden? No, the sprawling arms probably wouldn't like that. But the second clue was interesting: the leaves that were strewn across the floor...not that there were any mice or fleas in Minna's apartment, but surely it would feel nice to walk barefoot across scented leaves, wouldn't it?

Ping. Laryssa: **Have you seen Ado again?**

Yes.

And???

I didn't take a photo. That way you can picture him however you like.

Ellie sent a crying laughing emoji. She loved it when Caspia teased Laryssa like this.

She put the piece of paper with Ado's number in the envelope with Rosalind's letter. Why hadn't she given him her number as well? She was such an idiot. Now she was the one who had to text him!

Caspia sighed. But she still had a smile on her lips when she arrived outside of Mrs Wahid's shop.

The Fragrant Nymph

This time Mrs Wahid did not sit on her chair when Caspia entered the store. She stood at the top of a steep ladder resting against the shelves, organizing jars. It looked a bit dangerous, especially considering her age. Monyet sat at the bottom of the ladder as if he wanted to keep it from tipping over. He got up when he saw Caspia, but instead of barking at her, he just wagged his stubby little tail.

'You see?!' Mrs Wahid called down to her. 'I knew you two would become friends. How is your mother? I am sure she has invented a dozen new recipes since I last saw you.'

'Yes, and her spice shopping list is getting longer and longer.' Caspia reached for the ladder even though this earned her a disapproving look from Monyet. 'I think she'll end up buying up half your store.'

'Well, I hope I'll have everything she is looking for.' Mrs Wahid dusted one last jar on the shelf to her left and climbed down the ladder with astounding agility. 'So—what can I do for you today?'

Caspia forgot to respond for a moment. A small, warm body pressed against her legs. Monyet gave her an expectant look. *Come on, girl! Pet me. What are you waiting for?*

Could she trust him? Caspia patted the strong little body so carefully that Mrs Wahid laughed.

'Monyet is not made of porcelain, even though he has the right color for it. But I understand why you don't trust him. I am often unsure what goes on in that head of his. Try behind his ears.'

That was good advice. Monyet purred like a cat when Caspia scratched behind his pointed ears. He looked a little bit like a bat. A dog-bat.

'Mint. Today is all about mint,' she said. 'Is that also considered a spice? Or would it be better to buy it in tea bags? I need quite a lot.'

Mrs Wahid crossed her arms. 'Mint. Hm, how would I categorize it? A spice? Sometimes. But mint is so much more. What do you need it for? Cooking? Or does someone in your family have a cold? A few drops of mint oil into a cup of hot water and inhale the steam—nothing works better.'

But Caspia shook her head.

'I have this idea. But I need a lot of mint for it. I...' Maybe it was a bit weird.

'Out with it!' Mrs Wahid gave her an encouraging smile.

'I...want to spread the leaves on my floor. Like they did in the Middle Ages.'

'Ah, you have fleas in your room!' Mrs Wahid gave her an empathetic look. 'Or is it mice?'

'No!' Now Caspia really was embarrassed. 'I just like the idea of the feel of...'

'...scented leaves between your toes and of going to bed with feet that smell like mint. Oh what fun!' Mrs Wahid clapped her hands. 'Hmm. Well. Let me see. Hmm. You really will need a lot.'

She let her eyes roam the shelves. Then she pushed the ladder over to the one on the far left of the store. 'Do you see that large brown paper bag over there?' She pointed up toward the top shelf. 'Go ahead and grab two of those.'

The ladder really was very old. Caspia was surprised that Mrs Wahid had not broken her back climbing up the thin rungs yet.

'Yes, those are the right ones,' Mrs Wahid called up to

her. 'The content won't be enough to cover your whole floor, but you could strew a small path with it—between your bed and the door for example. Your feet will smell so good! And your room, too! Throw the bags down to me! You only need to pay for one of them, the other one is a gift!'

The bags were almost as big as Monyet, but not very heavy. Mrs Wahid caught them as skillfully as if she often received her spices this way. And Caspia was relieved that she did not have to carry them down the ladder.

The gray-green lump that Mrs Wahid shook out of the bag and onto the counter was barely recognizable as leaves.

'You'll be surprised by how much comes out of these bags,' she said. 'For tea and cooking you need better quality, ideally fresh mint, of course.'

The cash register with the golden dragon sounded a gentle ring when she opened it. It was the sort of cash register that they had in old movies. Very old movies. 'I used to have excellent mint in my yard,' said Mrs Wahid. 'But it overgrew everything, so I ended up turning it into tea. Oh well.' She shrugged her shoulders. 'We often only value what we have once we lose it. Humans can be quite foolish that way, don't you think?'

'I suppose so,' Caspia said, 'but I don't think you're foolish at all.'

Mrs Wahid gave her a wide smile as she handed over her change. 'Thank you very much! I take that as a great compliment. You don't strike me as at all foolish either. I really like our conversations. May I ask how old you are?'

'Twelve, well almost thirteen.'

'Twelve!' Mrs Wahid cried. 'All the bridges you will cross, all the doors you will open! You are still at the very beginning of the journey. Your whole life is still ahead of you. How exciting! Did you know that I left home at thirteen? Here that is seen as much too young, and maybe it is. The world moves so much faster today. But... I found my way, and so will you.'

Mrs Wahid squeezed one of the mint bags into Caspia's basket and helped her put the other one under her arm. Then she opened a drawer and chucked two tea bags into the basket as well. 'This is a very good mint tea. Not as good as fresh mint, but really not bad. Until next time.'

Mom was sleeping on the couch when Caspia got home. On the carpet next to her lay handwritten notes from one of her cooking classes. Caspia picked them up and covered her mother with a blanket she had found in the bedroom closet. It must have been Minna's handiwork as it was embroidered with dozens of flowers, all of them different.

On the kitchen table a note was tucked underneath the plate that Mom had prepared for her. *I did it! Hurray for my Bamboosle Noodles!*

She had indeed done it! Caspia ate two huge portions and nearly licked the plate clean. She had to think of the tamales that she had traded for apple soup. The memory made her smile once again. Her Brooklyn-life felt so full already although they had just arrived a few weeks ago. Did that happen in all new places? Surely in places where you met people like Mrs Wahid, Jemila, and Ado. And where you could eat Bamboosle Noodles!

Mrs Wahid's bags really did contain enough dried mint leaves to make a wide path in Caspia's room, leading from her bed to the dresser. They filled the room with their scent even before Caspia could slip out of her sandals and carefully set her bare feet down on the mint path. The dried leaves stuck to her skin, tickled between her toes, and wrapped her in fresh, spicy sweetness. As she walked up and down, she imagined herself to be a witch in a forest, with a fox sleeping next to her bed. During a time when there was no street noise like the one wafting up through her window.

She took a picture of the fragrant path for Ellie and Laryssa, but you could see nothing but gray-green leaves and the old wooden floorboards in it. *Sometimes the eyes really don't reveal very much at all, Rosalind,* Caspia thought as she took a picture of her foot covered in sticky leaves. If only I could send the scent as well!

Mint! she typed. Mint is the plant of the day!

A few minutes later Ellie sent her a passage of text:

MINTHE was a nymph from the mountain Mintha in Elis (southern Greece), loved by the god Hades. When she claimed to be superior to his wife Persephone, the furious goddess turned her into a mint plant… Mint was likely used in ancient burial rituals to cover the smell of the dead, and therefore became a sacred plant of Hades.

The smell of the dead? Caspia looked down at the dried leaves on her floor. Oh well…they smelled good anyway!

Laryssa wrote an hour later.

You still haven't sent a picture of Ado!

Rosalind's Seventh Letter

December 9, 1960

Dear, dear Minna,

Is it cold in Brooklyn? Is it snowing for you? Oh, I would love to catch snowflakes in my hands, but we are in Egypt. The mint handkerchief that you sent is the best protection against the warm desert wind. You added some drops of mint oil to your thread, did you not? Is it not wonderful that we can liquify scent? I only have to gently press the handkerchief to my nose and the enchanted nymph fills my head and lungs with her fresh odor. Long live Minthe!

The plant you have to guess today presents us with a very different gift. Papa and I discussed all night long whether I should really make it your next riddle. There is so much darkness connected to it, although of course that is not the plant's fault. It is so unique and great that in the end we decided to include it after all.

So...here are my clues:

1. The gift of warmth is associated with this plant, but also terrible cruelty and multitudes of pain.

2. It takes half a year to grow from seed to harvest.

3. Its white flowers turn red after they have been pollinated.

4. Aphids, caterpillars, and weevils...all kinds of insects enjoy its leaves, which is why it often gets sprayed with poison.

5. In a cave in Mexico, they found seven-thousand-year-old cloth that was made from it.

This plant will make a perfect model for your embroidery, Minna. It might even give you a little thread. Although unfortunately it is not true what they used to believe: that it is a tree with sheep growing on it.

I send you love as warm as the desert,
Your Rosalind

Bringer of Joy

The flowers that Jemila was arranging when Caspia stepped into the store were as yellow as if the sun that was warming the street outside had gotten caught between Jemila's fingers. Even the hairdressers had moved chairs onto the sidewalk to escape the heat inside their stores. And outside the café next door, a waiter was pouring water onto the roots of a young tree whose leaves had become limp between the parked cars. There were people everywhere who were in tune with the Green Kingdom.

'Hey, are you also half melted?' Jemila greeted her. 'Your roses are probably all wilted by now. We just got some old roses in today. Misleading name, I know,' she added with a laugh. 'That's what you call very special types of roses that have been around for a very, very long time. Look at them. Each blossom is as if you were peeking underneath a ballgown, with dozens of petticoats. And their names: La Reine, Empress Josephine, Chapeau de Napoléon!'

Caspia was impressed by how well the French names rolled off Jemila's tongue.

'What?' Jemila winked at her. 'I have Caribbean roots! We all speak French. And Spanish because my father's family is from Cuba.'

'You also have Nigerian roots. And South African ones,' the voice sounded from behind the curtain. Ah, Jemila's Zia was back.

Caribbean, Cuban, Nigerian, South African? She imagined traveling to all those places with Jemila. The world was so big. In Maine it was easy to forget that sometimes.

The scent of the old roses, as Jemila had called them, was heavy and sweet. Caspia had only ever seen roses like that in old paintings, and she had to admit that she had believed that the painters had just painted them wrong because they looked so different from modern roses! Jemila was right—with all their petals they really did look like ball gowns.

'They are probably really expensive, aren't they?' she asked as she ran her fingers over the buds of one that was the pale pink of a blushing cheek.

Jemila glanced at the curtain.

'SO expensive!' she whispered. 'But you could have some of the ones that are fully open already. They won't last much longer anyway, and customers would only complain if we sold them.'

'Forget it. I don't want to get you in trouble,' Caspia whispered back and took Rosalind's letter from her basket. 'I opened the next envelope. Listen to the clues: "The gift of warmth is associated with this plant, but also terrible cruelty and multitudes of pain. It takes half a year to grow from seed to harvest. Its white flowers turn red after they have been pollinated. Aphids, weevils, caterpillars...all kinds of insects enjoy its leaves, which is why it often gets sprayed with poison." And—I think this one gives it away: "In a cave in Mexico they found seven-thousand-year-old cloth that was made from it." What do you think?'

Jemila put a yellow flower into the bouquet she was arranging. 'Cotton. Definitely.'

'Exactly, that's what I thought. I googled the flowers and it's true, they really do change color! Isn't that bizarre?'

'Yeah, bizarre.' Jemila put another flower into the bouquet. 'Have I ever told you that one of my ancestors picked cotton in the fields of South Carolina? I think it was my great-great-great-grandmother.'

The gift of warmth is associated with this plant, but also terrible cruelty and multitudes of pain. How could she have been so stupid? Caspia was so ashamed. She had been so absorbed in solving Rosalind's riddle. And she had been so looking forward to seeing Jemila and spending time in her magical store that she... *Oh stop it, Caspia, there is no excuse.*

Jemila was not looking at her, but just continued to arrange the flowers. 'She was from Nigeria,' Jemila said. 'Her brother was captured and taken away, too. He died on the ship, but she survived the crossing and...well, then it was nothing but picking cotton! In a foreign country. From sunrise to sunset.'

'I am so sorry. I'm so thoughtless,' Caspia mumbled. 'I...'

'Nope!' Jemila raised her head and looked at her. 'I am pretty sure it wasn't one of your ancestors who dragged her to his cotton fields. So that her bloody hands would make him rich. Or do you happen to have a slave trader or plantation owner in your family?'

Caspia's eyes widened in shock. 'I... I don't know!'

'I prefer this version of the story.' Jemila collected a few cut-off flower stems from the counter. 'One of your ancestors fell in love with my great-great-great-grandmother, after she escaped the plantation where they held her. But she didn't want him because his pale Scottish skin turned as red as lobster meat in the sun.'

Her laugh was as bright as the yellow flowers, and Caspia simply had to join in. Even though she was ashamed that her ignorance had forced Jemila to build this bridge of words over an abyss of pain. An abyss that she had so thoughtlessly forgotten over a riddle. But she very much liked the idea that one of her ancestors had been in love with Jemila's great-great-great-grandmother.

Jemila walked over to the vase with the old roses and pulled out three whose blossoms were open so wide that they looked like flowery hands, reaching for the sun. 'You can't change the past, and neither can I,' she said. 'And it's still happening! Everywhere! We can only try to be friends.'

'Yes, please. Very best friends,' Caspia said. 'But my skin also turns red in the sun.'

Jemila wrapped the roses in pale-green paper. 'Yeah, it probably looks pretty terrible. And my Zia already thinks that you're only distracting me from work.' She shrugged her shoulders. 'I think the two of us are a pretty good team anyway. You can prove it right now.'

She pointed toward the bouquet she had just put together. 'What vase would this look best in?'

Caspia looked at all the vases that stood on the shelf behind the counter. *And it's still happening! Everywhere!*

We can only try to be friends. Yes. Caspia could already barely imagine not having Jemila in her life. They really were such a good team.

'I think that one would look fantastic.' She pointed toward a bulbous vase of violet blue porcelain.

'There you go. I would have picked the same one.' Jemila took the vase off the shelf and filled it with water. Then she arranged the flowers one last time—and handed them to Caspia. 'Put it with the others. You can choose a spot.' Caspia sat down the vase next to a flagon of blue irises—yes, those she knew because Dad always got them for Mom on her birthday.

'Perfect. Now we just have to find the right book to put next to them.' Jemila stepped up to the shelves and browsed the spines of the books. Then she pulled one out and handed it to Caspia, along with a silver book stand.

'Friendship plants,' Caspia read. She gave Jemila a grateful smile. Then she put the stand with the book next to the yellow flowers and took a picture.

'What was her name?' she asked. 'The name of your ancestor.'

'Abeke. I looked it up. It means Bringer of Joy.'

Jemila surveyed the flower arrangement in the window and moved the irises a little to the right. 'Do you know your great-great-great-grandfather' name?'

Caspia shook her head.

'All right, he needs a name then...' Jemila frowned and looked up at the ceiling as if Caspia's ancestor would whisper his name from that direction. 'Timothy! Yes. Timothy fell in love with Abeke and when she didn't return his love, he ran all the way to Maine to cool down his burning heart.'

They laughed so hard that Caspia tripped against one of the displays. Jemila reached for her arm, but the vase on top of the stand shattered on the floor.

They hastily crouched down next to the shards and gathered them up along with the flowers that had been inside.

'Dahlias,' Jemila whispered, as she wiped up the water. 'Not my favorite flower. They look sort of like they're made of plastic.'

They both turned a worried eye toward the curtain, but it stayed quiet. Jemila crept up to it on her tiptoes and carefully peeked behind it. Then she tilted her head to the side and put both hands under her cheek as if she was sleeping.

'Zia played Bingo with her friends last night,' she whispered. 'It must have been a late one.'

They started giggling again until Caspia was gasping for breath.

'I'll try to order a cotton plant,' Jemila said when all the shards had been cleaned up and the dahlias had a new vase. 'And then we'll explore it with our fingers and noses just like Rosalind.'

She went to the counter and handed Caspia the wrapped roses. 'These ones are called Great Maiden's Blush. You wouldn't believe the names they used to give roses. Many you couldn't even say out loud anymore!'

Caspia reached for her wallet.

But Jemila shook her head. 'Like I said. They're a gift. I can't sell them anyway. And I'm sure my aunt won a ton of money at Bingo last night. She always has good luck gambling.'

There was a rustling sound behind the curtain.

'It might be best if you go now!' Jemila hissed. 'I have to get back to work. Or Zia will cut me like a long flower stem.'

Caspia obeyed.

Oh, I'll miss Jemila! she thought, as she closed the door of *Blooms & Books* behind her. *So much.*

But at least for now she was still here!

Cotton

Rosalind's Eighth Letter

February 17, 1961

Late night greetings from Glasgow, Minna!

Yes, we are back home, where your embroidered cotton plant was waiting for me. The fluffy seeds almost fooled my fingers. They really feel like those of a living plant. I also discovered the tears you let fall from the leaves, and the terrible chain out of which the plant is growing. What a powerful image, Minna! Papa put it next to the embroidery you made of my favorite bird, the hoopoe, who always flies away before I can grasp it. Only your embroidery gives me the chance to touch it. They are both on the wall next to my bed now.

But now...here is the next riddle. It is the eighth if I have counted correctly. This time, Minna, you have to guess a plant that is considered sacred in many parts of the world. That is your first clue!

Here are the others:

2. When you fall asleep under it, it is possible you will wake up in the faery realm.

3. Great wands can be crafted from its wood, but you have to ask for permission before cutting one of its branches, otherwise it will have its revenge.

4. A bath with its flowers can heal bad rashes.

5. The ancient Romans made a wine from its berries and used the brew to dye their hair black.

Well, has it already enchanted you? I am sure you will know its name soon. And please do not curse me for having picked this plant. It will probably not be easy to embroider with its countless tiny flowers and berries. Oh no, now I have given away too much again, haven't I?

When you find it, don't fall asleep under its branches, Minna!

I send you all my love!
Rosalind

Growth

Wands, a hair dye, waking up in the faery realm? Tiny berries AND flowers. Caspia didn't think that Rosalind had given away the answer to her eighth riddle at all. On the contrary, she did not have the slightest idea what the answer might be.

It was Ellie who found it. Although she admitted that a librarian named Linda with a weakness for Irish folklore had helped her. Linda had confided in Ellie that as a child she had really tried to reach the faery realm by sleeping under an elder tree. Residence of the mystical Lady Elder, who Caspia had found in two stories in Jemila's books.

Laryssa immediately tested the fifth clue on her little brother's hair. But because her parents didn't want to donate a bottle of wine to the endeavor, she only managed to dye her own hands and his face dark red. Ellie was as fascinated by the second clue as Linda the librarian, and stole out of the house that very evening to sleep underneath the elder tree in her backyard—which did not end well because her mother caught her and absolutely refused to believe that the whole thing had been about the faery realm.

According to the website, the Brooklyn Botanic Garden actually housed multiple black elder trees.

Will you tell Ado that you're going? Laryssa asked before Caspia had even had a chance to consider it.

Ellie commented with the observation that Laryssa once again overestimated the importance of boys in life. To which Laryssa shot back that just because Ellie didn't care about boys didn't mean the rest of them weren't allowed to. And why wasn't Ellie more interested anyway?

Ellie did not reply.

Laryssa apologized but Ellie remained quiet. And Caspia suddenly regretted that she was so far away. Keeping the peace between the two of them was often her job in this friendship. But she WAS far away...

Ellie continued to stay silent. She also didn't respond to Caspia's message asking if she was all right. She had probably buried her cell phone under some pillow, like Ellie always did when she didn't want to talk about something.

After Caspia had texted her one more time, she poured herself a mug of the elderberry tea she had found in one of Mom's tea cans, and then...yes, then...

Don't be a coward, Caspia! she believed she could hear Rosalind whisper. Why not? Yes, she would send Ado a message.

If she found his number...

She searched her wallet and the basket she always had with her. But there was no sign of the piece of paper with his number on it. She was almost sure she had lost it when she remembered that she had tucked it into the envelope with Rosalind's letter. But which one had it been? The fourth? The fifth? No! Mint. That was...number six!

By now there were two stacks of letters in the dresser drawer—on the left, the letters she had already opened, on the right, the ones that were still waiting to be read. There were only two left—and they would be in Brooklyn for another eight weeks. Caspia was surprised to find that the thought that they ONLY had eight more weeks made her a little sad. How quickly thoughts and feelings could change. It was a little confusing. Maybe she should save the last two letters and not open the next one for at least another three weeks. Hmmm. She'd leave that decision for later.

Cinnamon, dandelion, rose, bamboo, apple...yes! Mint was number six, and inside the envelope alongside Rosalind's letter, was the piece of paper that Ado had torn from his sketchbook.

Would he think that she had a crush on him if she texted him? *You DO have a crush on him, Caspia,* she could hear Laryssa say. No! They were friends. Laryssa was convinced that friendship was impossible between boys and girls, but she really was not as highly qualified an expert as she liked to believe.

Hi, Caspia started typing. **It's me, Caspia, the one with the letters.**

That sounded pretty lame, didn't it?

I'll be at the BBG on Sunday to take a look at the elder trees. I'll bring the next letter as well. Would you like to come?

Caspia hit send before she could change her mind. She had to admit that she was pretty pleased with herself. Did new places make you braver? Did growing new roots make you stronger? No, it made you strong to know that you could!

Before she left, she tried to reach Ellie one more time.

Hey, she texted. **Are you okay?**

This time Ellie responded.

Yes! she texted and added a little black heart. Ellie loved little black hearts. **Laryssa came by. She cycled over on her brother's bike.**

Laryssa hated riding bikes. Ellie knew that, of course. Laryssa must have been in a hurry to make things right.

I told her I like girls, Ellie wrote, **and she said she loves me no matter what. She almost ran my dad over barging into the house.** Ellie added three crying laughing emojis. **She is so ridiculous! And she misses you as much as I do. We both can't wait for you to come back.**

Caspia sent back three golden hearts. What would Ellie have said had she known that she was starting to put down roots in Brooklyn? Brooklyn of all places! How could they ever make fun of tourists from New York again?

She took her tea and went to her room to check on the plants. The nasturtium already had two tiny leaves and the dandelion was growing so fast you could almost watch it. And that was despite the fact that she still had to get proper pots for them.

Would Ado come?

She looked at her phone. He hadn't responded yet.

How had Rosalind known when she liked a boy? Had his voice been the deciding factor? Or had she read their faces with her fingers, too? *Well, that would definitely take a lot more courage than sending a text, Caspia,* she thought, as she carried the roses into the kitchen to give them fresh water.

Mom was sitting at the table, once again working on her spice wish list for Mrs Wahid's store. She had filled two full pages of printer paper by now.

'No comment please!' she said when Caspia looked over her shoulder. 'I have to buy all these spices here because I can't get them at home! Can you believe that we've almost been here for a month already? The time has gone by so fast, hasn't it? I'll probably even miss the floral wallpapers when we're back in Maine.'

'Yeah, me too,' Caspia mumbled. She would miss many things. No Mrs Wahid around the corner anymore, no Jemila, no adventures in the Botanic Garden with Ado...and no letters from Rosalind. Just a few weeks ago none of those things had meant anything to her. Let alone cinnamon or elder trees.

'But we'll be here for another eight weeks,' Mom said. 'When that's over, I am sure we'll be homesick.'

Maybe. Caspia filled the vase with water and put the old roses back inside. They were starting to lose their petals but they still smelled so good.

How quickly thoughts and feelings could change...

Maybe it also had to do with her finding the letters of

a girl who had loved to travel? Were Rosalind's letters—even more so than Brooklyn—the reason that she suddenly asked herself who exactly she was and where she belonged? Plants handed their seeds over to the wind and reinvented themselves over and over again in new places. Oh, Caspia wished that she could talk about all this with Rosalind.

'What dish would you think of with elderflower, Mom?'

'Elderflower? One of your Dad's aunts used to make a liqueur from it and claimed that it was the best medicine against pretty much everything. I've only ever made jam from the berries and...' she pointed toward Caspia's mug, '... tea from the flowers. I am afraid you can only find the fresh flowers in spring. But I could try making something with the berries. Something more exciting than jam?'

'Sounds good!'

Mom ran her finger over her eyebrow in thought. She often did that when she was trying to come up with something. 'Elderberries...hmmm. Getting those probably won't be easy either. But I accept the challenge. I'll miss these riddles. Who is posting them again? Or is that a secret?'

Okay, Caspia! Mom would surely understand that she could not give back the letters before having read the last two. Caspia took a deep breath. She really had no practice at all keeping secrets from her parents.

'It is true that they were posted,' she began carefully. 'In some way. Just in the old-fashioned way. I mean...they're letters, Mom.'

Without the ribbon and the dried flower, Rosalind's letters did not look quite as romantic anymore. Caspia put both down next to the stack of letters that she had already read, before adding the last two envelopes with slight hesitation. Mom definitely wouldn't return all the letters before she could read the last two, would she?

Mom pulled the cinnamon tree letter from its envelope. She read the dandelion letter and the rose letter. Then she laid out those three next to each other on the kitchen table and looked at the other envelopes.

'You found such a wonderful thing on our first day here?' she asked. 'Without showing them to me or your Dad? Caspia Turkel, what else are you hiding from us?'

'Nothing, Mom!' Caspia protested.

Although...

'I also met some new friends,' she added.

'Friends aren't a secret,' Mom said. 'And it's completely fine if you don't tell us everything. Have I ever told you about how your grandmother used to read my journal? She didn't even feel bad when I finally caught her one day.'

'That's terrible!' Caspia cried, even though she had never had the desire to keep a journal herself.

'Yes, that it was,' Mom said. 'What's the point of a journal if you can't trust it with your most secret and embarrassing thoughts?'

She read all the letters—except for the two that Caspia hadn't read yet. Then she regarded the floral wallpaper with a smile.

'Now all the flowers make sense,' she said. 'They reminded Minna of her little sister and her father. And all the embroidered oven mitts that are so beautiful I don't even dare use them...those are Minna's handiwork! She was an artist with a needle!'

She helped Caspia put the letters back in the right envelopes and wrapped the ribbon around the ones that had already been opened. Mom even managed to reattach the dried flower. 'We really should give them to the landlady,' she said. 'After you've read the last two, of course.' With a smile, she held the two envelopes out to Caspia. 'Can we open the next one together?'

Caspia blushed. Had she blushed so much in Maine? It was annoying.

'I... I was actually planning on doing that with Ado. He's one of my new friends.'

'Ado...' Mom gave her a searching look as if she had just discovered something new about her. Something that had not been there until now. 'I think we have to plan regular visits to Brooklyn from now on, don't you think?'

'Yes. But we always have to...'

'...stay in this apartment,' Mom finished her sentence. 'Yes, I think so too. And I should probably start thinking about an elderberry recipe!'

Caspia noticed Ado's response when she was taking the roses back to her room.

There's a big elder tree in the water garden. Should we meet there?

Caspia replied with a smiley face and a thumbs-up.

She felt so warm and happy that she simply had to share the feeling.

Ado says there's an elder tree in the water garden, she wrote to Ellie and Laryssa.

You know what, Ellie wrote back. **I'm sure it was my wristband that brought Ado into the pavilion with the cinnamon tree when Caspia was there.**

That is the silliest, most superstitious nonsense I have ever read! Laryssa commented. **That's a record even for you, Ellie!**

Yes, it was all back to normal between those two. Caspia sighed with relief.

You know what Ellie?!! Laryssa loved exclamation points. **Even your wristband won't protect Caspia from my wrath if she doesn't finally send us a picture of Ado tomorrow!**

I will definitely not be doing that, Caspia wrote back. **I'll just make myself a wand from elder wood to protect me.**

Dad was a little more upset than Mom had been that Caspia hadn't told them about the letters sooner. And he asked a thousand questions about Ado, which Caspia found a little irritating.

Dad had brought another plant from the construction site. It was butterfly weed, as they found out together. *Asclepias tuberosa* was a very important plant for several species of butterfly. Which made Dad even more proud for saving it.

They all went to bed kind of early that night, but Caspia had a hard time falling asleep. Too many thoughts and feelings filled her head and heart.

You're just excited because you have a date! Laryssa wrote when she saw that Caspia was still online at midnight.

But that wasn't true—even though Caspia was really

looking forward to seeing Ado. There was so much more. She listened to the city noise that wafted in through the open window. *You're just growing some new leaves, Caspia,* she thought, *like the young dandelion and the nasturtium.* But it was strange, suddenly having new thoughts and feelings. Would she be the old Caspia again when they went back home? Did she just have a different color in Brooklyn? The flowers Mom loved so much—hydrangeas. They changed their color depending on which soil they grew in.

Eventually she fell asleep. And dreamed. Of fairies, that looked exactly like the ones from Ellie's old fairytale book that she had photographed and sent to her. They floated above the Botanic Garden, with elderflowers that they held over their heads like white parasols.

Elderflower

The Fairy Bush

'Here. I brought you something.' The flowers that Ado held out to Caspia were bright orange, and their scent laced the air with the colors of the south.

'Mexican honeysuckle,' he said. 'It grows everywhere in our backyard. My father believes that its scent spreads joy. Even on sad days.'

Caspia found this very easy to believe. Although she was sure that today she was not only happy because of the honeysuckle but also because of Ado.

'They're beautiful,' she said as she buried her nose in the flowers, because this was a great way to hide that she was blushing once again.

The water garden was her favorite place in the BBG so far. There was a running brook and a pond—and a large elder tree spread its branches as if it was welcoming them.

Caspia stepped closer to the tree and ran her hands over the dark berries that hung off the branches by the dozen, like umbrellas heavy with rain. Mom was right. She would have to wait for elderflowers until next spring. The dark green leaves rustled in the wind, and for a moment, the story with the fairies did not sound all that improbable.

'Your father is right,' she whispered to Ado. 'Plants speak. This one most definitely does. Can you hear it?'

'Of course.' Ado was in the process of inspecting one of the branches. 'Look. This one would make a great flute. Or a wand. Wasn't that one of the clues?' He sighed. 'Unfortunately, my father would rip off my head if I cut as much as a single branch off his precious bushes. He considers himself the protector of all the plants here.'

Caspia found that very comforting. She liked Ado's father already.

'I read in a friend's book that witches used to summon storms with elder,' she said. 'They would hollow out a branch and stir water with it until they awakened the wind.'

'Interesting.' Ado surveyed the elder tree. 'Should we try it?'

'Definitely not!' Caspia caught herself throwing a worried glance up at the sky. But it was a reassuring blue. Was she becoming as superstitious as Ellie?

Ado winked at her. 'I'm sure my father knows how to talk to elder trees. I will ask him to cut a branch for us. Just a very small one. It can't hurt to have a wand, can it? And I wanted to introduce you to my father anyway.'

You could tell from looking at him that Ado's father had spent the majority of his life outdoors. His face was as weather-worn as the bark of an old tree, and he seemed to watch the world with similar serenity. Like a tree. Or like Rosalind... Maybe plants taught you things that couldn't be learned in buildings or on tarmacked streets?

'Ah, Caspia! I have heard a lot about you,' he greeted her with a smile. 'The girl with the green riddles. What plant brings you here today?'

His grin broadened further when Caspia told him.

'Elder... I used to cut wands from its wood. Because you can be sure with elder that it will only cast good magic.'

Ado exchanged a look with Caspia. *You see?* his eyes seemed to say. *We'll get our wand.*

'There are two more growing behind the tool shed,' his father continued. 'The berries have healed many a cold in the Baldenegro family. And of course they also provide sustenance for many non-human inhabitants of this garden.'

One of the trees growing behind the tool shed was almost as big as the one in the water garden. Ado's father spoke to it in Spanish before cutting one of the smaller branches with his garden clippers and handing it to Caspia with a smile.

'For you. To protect you on your plant adventure.'

'Oh, thank you!' Caspia ran her fingers over the bark. 'Thank you very, very much. Do you think it would root if I planted it?'

In one spot, tiny, fresh leaves were sprouting from the bark.

Señor Baldenegro smiled. 'Ah, spoken like a true gardener! Try it. Stick it in some good soil and water it regularly, maybe before long you will have a young elder tree.'

These days that sounded much more interesting to Caspia than a wand. 'Do you have a favorite plant, Señor Baldenegro?' she asked.

'Hmmm.' Ado's father closed his eyes for a moment as if he had to recall all the plants he loved. 'Ah, I know! The ahuehuete tree,' he said, opening his eyes again with a smile. 'It is full of laughter and stories. Its name means *old man of the water*. They have declared it the national tree of Mexico, but the ahuehuete isn't really interested in such honorifics.'

He pointed toward the elder branch that he had cut for Caspia. 'You should wrap it in wet paper if you want to plant it. So it doesn't forget that it is a plant. And now the compost requires my attention. To make new earth from plant cuttings, leftover vegetables and coffee grounds...all these gifts that so many just throw away...that is my favorite kind of magic. And you do not even need a wand for it.' He winked at his son. 'Ado thinks compost is disgusting since he fell into a heap of it that was still ripening, and his clothes were suddenly teeming with worms and centipedes. It did not help either when I told them they are my most precious helpers.'

Ado shuddered and looked down at his clothes as if he was worried he would discover a few more of those helpers there. 'I spent days smelling like compost, Dad!'

'That is the smell of life,' his father retorted. 'You will miss it one day, when the world smells of nothing but car exhaust. Nothing will ever grow from that, that's for sure.'

Caspia would have liked to hear more about Señor Baldenegro's little helpers. But Ado kept looking at her backpack.

It was time to solve Rosalind's next riddle.

Rosalind's Ninth Letter

May 23, 1961

Dear Minna,

The elderflower oven mitts are brilliant and very practical proof of you having solved my eighth riddle. Of course you have not forgotten how often Papa burns his fingers when he cooks. He is so embarrassed that it hardly ever happens to me. But from now on Lady Elder will protect him.

Only two more plants, Minna, and Papa will send you a plane ticket so that we can finally embrace each other once more. I can hardly wait to hear your voice! But because we love our green riddles so much by now—what do you think of Papa's idea to continue our game after your visit with ten embroidered riddles? Which, of course, would mean that you have to think of them this time. I do hope your answer is YES?!!

But for now, here is the ninth plant that you have to guess. Many hate and curse it. But those who know the secrets of the Green Kingdom consider it one of its most fascinating citizens.

Here are the clues:

1. Roman soldiers used to whip their own skin with it to prepare for battle and some of North America's indigenous peoples used to do the same in order to gain strength and protection before hunting dangerous game.

2. The Brothers Grimm tell of a girl who knit six shirts from this plant to free her brothers from a curse that had turned them into swans.

3. The leaves can dye cloth a yellow almost as bright as dandelion flowers.

4. The young leaves help against arthritis and asthma, and in the Middle Ages it was believed that it could cure baldness—which has unfortunately turned out to not be true.

5. The Cherokee address it as 'my friend' to protect themselves from its burn.

Do you recognize the steady companion of our childhood? Even though we never sought out its company, it always seemed to be there, teaching us respect whenever we forgot about it by burning our naked legs. I have to put it in the fridge before I can touch it.

Perhaps I better do the same with your embroidered portrait, just to make sure that it will not sting my fingers?

I send you all my love from Hamburg, where this plant seems to feel just as at home as it does in Scotland!

Your Rosalind

Ghosts and Gray Stones

'Swans!' Caspia looked up from Rosalind's letter. 'I know that fairytale! The girl doesn't manage to finish the last shirt, and her youngest brother has a swan wing for an arm for the rest of his life.'

'Wow.' Ado surveyed his left arm as if he was disappointed to find it was not a wing. 'So? Which plant is it?'

Caspia looked at her cell phone. Yes, the fairytale had given her the right answer. 'It's the stinging nettle!' she said. 'Roman soldiers lashed their skin with it because it increases blood circulation. That prepared them for battle, but it also made the cold more bearable during their conquests of Germany and Britain.' She looked around. 'As a kid I always used to stumble into them, but I guess we won't find one in a Botanic Garden, will we?'

'Oh yes. My father made a spot for them behind the greenhouses where they can grow unencumbered,' Ado said. 'He makes fertilizer from them. The stuff smells absolutely terrible but he swears it's better than any artificial fertilizer.'

'Fantastic,' Caspia said. 'I just have to take a photo of them.'

But Ado shook his head. 'I think we should find nettles somewhere else.' He lowered his voice. 'What do you think of a cemetery for a change?'

When Caspia looked at him in surprise, Ado pointed toward the letter in her lap. 'I found out where Minna's grave is.'

Of course! Caspia could not believe that it had never occurred to her that Minna was most likely buried in Brooklyn. Maybe because she always imagined Rosalind and her older sister as young as they were in the letters.

'Would you like to visit her?' Ado asked. 'Or do you prefer to stay away from cemeteries? Mexicans usually like them but...'

'I like them, too,' Caspia said. 'I was just...'

'...you're wondering if Rosalind will be there too,' Ado finished her sentence. He already knew her well. Caspia was almost tempted to take a picture of him after all. 'Yeah,' she murmured. 'Yeah, you're right. What if she's there as well? How will that feel?'

At least she already knew that Minna had died. And the idea of visiting her grave was strange anyway.

'She's buried in the Green Wood Cemetery,' Ado said. 'Like my grandmother. It's nice up there. We drive there every year for Día de los Muertos, to sing for Abuela and bring her all of her favorite dishes.'

All of that you definitely did not do in cemeteries in Maine. It sounded more like what Rosalind and her father did on her mother's death-day.

'You can even see the Statue of Liberty from there!' Ado continued. 'And I'm sure there will be some nettles there somewhere. But maybe you shouldn't touch those with your eyes closed like you like to do?'

Caspia had to laugh even though she still felt slightly queasy about it. 'I just have to put them in the fridge first, then they don't sting.'

One hour and many steps and streets later they stood on the top of the world—at least it felt that way. Around them Green Wood Cemetery spread its green cloak, lined by the skyline of Brooklyn.

'Okay.' Ado pulled out his cell phone while Caspia let her eyes wander over all the gray tombstones and the white mausoleums.

'Green Wood Cemetery...' Ado read, '...was founded in 1838. No planes, no cars and definitely no cell phones like this little magic device telling me all this.' He perched on one of the tombstones. Were you allowed to do that? Ado certainly seemed to think so.

'Green Wood has more than half a million residents. A real city of the dead. Around five thousand of those are soldiers from the Civil War.'

He leaned forward and looked at the tombstone on which he was sitting.

'Ava Bloom. 1842—1857. She died far too young,' he read out loud. 'That's true. Hello, Ava. I'm Ado, and this is Caspia.' He pointed to the right. 'I think Minna's grave is that way. She made it all the way to ninety. I think I'd be happy with that age.'

Ninety. Yes, Caspia was relieved to hear that.

It took them a while to find Minna's name, even though they kept looking at the cemetery's grave map. But there were thousands of grave markers, and all of them looked fairly similar, only the mausoleums and a few graves with statues stood out. The stone they eventually found was very beautiful, with rough edges and a kneeling angel carved into it.

The inscription on the stone read:

MINNA REYNOLDS

HER VOICE WILL BE MISSED

APRIL 13, 1932–DECEMBER 16, 2022

'We are lucky she kept her last name,' Ado said. 'Otherwise, we never would have found her.'

'She had a daughter. She's our landlady, but maybe Minna was never married.' Caspia knelt down in front of the grave. It was covered in small blue flowers. *Forget-me-nots.* She knew those from the grave of her great-grandmother. Her father's family had come to Wilmerton more than a hundred and fifty years ago, but he was the only descendent who still lived there now.

'Someone is taking care of the grave. These were planted quite recently,' Ado observed.

Someone... A bouquet of fresh wildflowers lay next to the stone. Something had been written on the wide green ribbon holding it together.

For Minna from Rosalind.

'You see?' Ado said. 'Of course she's still alive.'

Caspia was so relieved. Rosalind was alive. That was both a strange and a wonderful thought. Rosalind had likely also chosen the words for Minna's stone. Of course she would remember her sister's voice above all else.

Ado peeked behind the tombstone.

'And look at who the cemetery gardeners missed!' he

said and pulled his sleeve down over his hand. Then he reached behind the stone. When he straightened back up, he was holding a stinging nettle.

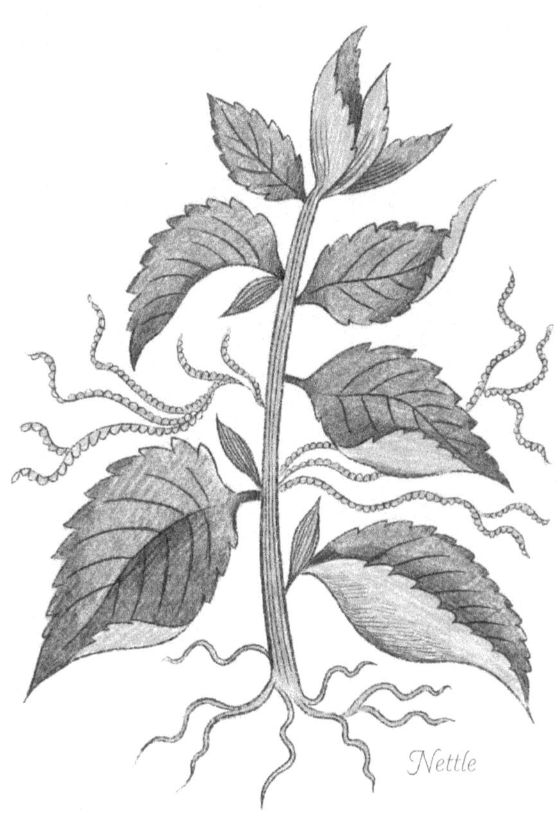

Just One More Letter

Mom made a jelly from elderberry juice—it was a sensation. Just like the soup she magicked from fresh nettles two days later.

'Good, this is the proof,' she said as Dad filled his plate for the third time. 'I am a pretty good chef! Can you two please remind me of that when we're back home and my mother makes fun of my cookbook project again?'

'Yes! I swear on all my plants!' Caspia said.

The elder branch now also sat on her windowsill, proud and strong, in one of the clay pots she had finally bought.

'Perfect,' Mom said. 'Because I'm afraid that as soon as we are back, I'll convince myself that I'm naive to think I can handle a book like that.'

And then they were all suddenly very quiet…as if none of them wanted to think about their return. Only seven more weeks…

'You only have one more letter, right?' Dad asked into the silence after a while. 'So, I guess we'll have to come up with our own green riddles for the rest of our stay.'

'Good idea,' Caspia said.

'I'll go first!' Mom said. 'I'll cook something and you two have to guess what plant gives the dish its name.'

'Sounds delicious!' Caspia said. 'I think I'll give you guys five clues, just like Rosalind. But I'll try to make them rhyme.'

'Not bad either!' Dad said. 'How about I press a leaf into cement, and you have to guess the plant based on the impression?'

'Wow!' Caspia sighed. 'That will be pretty difficult. But all right. We'll try it.'

And she would save all the impressions and take them back to Maine with her. Seven more weeks…would they continue with the riddles at home? Mom had the bold plan to convince Grandma to turn her huge lawn into a wild meadow. And she wanted to start a vegetable garden. She had just signed up for a class with the promising name *From the Backyard to the Plate*.

It was Dad who said out loud what none of them wanted to admit. He had always been good at that. 'This summer turned out to be a real adventure. And we're all a bit down because it will be over so soon, aren't we?'

Mom and Caspia nodded. 'True!'

They looked at each other, surrounded by Minna's floral, slightly faded wallpaper, at her old table where she had surely sat with Rosalind on more than one occasion.

'Jack says he doesn't like to see me go at all,' Dad said. 'He just got a job on a new construction site. Right on the river!'

He sighed.

'And there are so many more cooking classes I would like to take,' Mom said. And sighed as well.

Caspia stared at her empty plate.

'You've come around to Brooklyn as well, haven't you, Cass?' Dad asked. 'I know you weren't thrilled about coming here. But now you seem to be really happy. Are you still looking forward to going home? Ellie and Laryssa are probably counting the days already.'

'That they are,' Caspia said and ran her fingers over a split in Minna's old table. She hadn't told Ellie and Laryssa anything about her excursion to the cemetery yet. She and Ado had taken a selfie in front of the Minerva statue, the monument that stood at the highest point of the cemetery with its hand raised, as if it was waving at the statue of liberty. Ado had told her that George Washington, the first president of the United States, had lost a battle there. The pictures had turned out quite nice. And yes, she would send it to Laryssa. And Jemila and Ellie.

'I wish we had adventures like this more often,' she said. 'I want us to travel together. And get to know new places!'

Her parents exchanged a look.

'I like that plan,' Mom said.

'But...' Dad began.

'No buts,' Caspia interrupted him.

'All right then, no buts,' Dad said with a smile. 'Can we go get ice cream for dessert?'

Rosalind's Tenth Letter

November 14, 1961

Dear Minna,

I love your embroidered stinging nettle! It tickles my fingertips. If only I had your patience with needle and thread! Although... Papa just brought me some clay for sculpting... That is probably a safer material for me. You can make impressions of twigs, nuts, and fruits in it... I am so enchanted by it that my hands are crusted with clay all day.

But... now it is time for your final green riddle.
Before I pass on the job to you and your needle.

This citizen of our favorite kingdom has been praised in countless poems, and plays a part in stories all over the world. If I had to choose a favorite plant, Minna, I might well choose this one.

So, here it is:

1. People also call her the Queen of the Night.

2. A pillow filled with its flowers is said to keep away bad dreams.

3. The scent of its flowers can best be captured when you collect them in the early morning.

4. Many gods of love and desire wrap its vines around their bows before they aim for human hearts.

5. Its leaves contain the same substance that makes aspirin such a good pain medication.

I am very tempted to infuse this letter with the scent distilled from the flowers of my beautiful unknown, but that would really make it too easy. I await your portrait, Minna!

I am so excited to find out which plant you will choose for your first riddle!

With all my love, as always,
Your Rosalind

New Roots

The display window of *Blooms & Books* had already changed again. Caspia stood outside admiring it for quite a while before she stepped into the store to say hello to Jemila. Every gap between the vases and book stands was filled with small potted plants. Most of them Caspia knew from Mrs Wahid's courtyard: rosemary with its thick, needly twigs, silver-green sage and chives that were so easy to mistake for chunky grass.

'Do you like my new decoration?' Jemila asked. 'They're all herbs used in the kitchen. I asked Mrs Wahid for advice about them.'

'You know Mrs Wahid?'

Jemila raised an eyebrow in amusement. 'Of course I know her. Brooklyn is a village! An enchanted forest made of bricks and eccentric people.'

She stepped up next to Caspia and surveyed her

arrangement with a frown. Then she closed her eyes like Rosalind would have done and took a deep breath. 'My aunt was worried that the herbs would ruin the scent of the flowers, but I like it. As if we mixed together pepper and sugar.'

'I like it too.' Caspia took a picture of the new window and sent it to Laryssa and Ellie.

'Rosemary...' Jemila ran her fingers over the firm needles. '*Salvia rosmarinus*. I read yesterday that the name has nothing to do with roses. It derives from a Latin word that means ocean dew. Isn't that interesting? It's also a plant of remembrance. I think I'll write into my will that I want rosemary planted on my grave. And of course, an old rose.' She gave Caspia a conspiratorial wink. 'I saw the pictures you posted of Green Wood Cemetery. You were in good company!'

Laryssa had responded to the pictures with so many comments that Caspia had ignored them so far.

'Yes, very good,' she said. 'But can we talk about something else?'

'Sure.' Jemila took one of the fairytale books off its stand in the window and replaced it with *My Herb Garden and Its Stories*. Mom would have been very interested in that one.

'This window only gets better and better, don't you think?' Jemila draped her arm around Caspia's shoulders.

She smiled like a cat in the sun. 'We get new customers coming in every day! My aunt is very happy. Even though at first, she hated my idea to put the books in between the plants. She's out with one of her friends,' she added with a glance at the curtain. 'She leaves me in charge of the store more and more now.'

You could tell how much Jemila liked that.

With the herb pots, the window almost looked as if the vases were in a forest—where you could find books between the trees. Well, paper was usually made from trees, so they really belonged together anyway.

'I wish I could shrink myself and live in your display,' Caspia said.

Jemila laughed. 'As long as you're the size of a mouse, you're welcome any time. Did you see what just arrived?'

She pulled Caspia to the counter.

A colorful pot stood on top. The plant inside sprouted fluffy bolls between its dark green leaves. A cotton plant! Caspia gently stroked the soft cocoon that harbored the seeds. They really did look like cotton balls!

'I told my aunt I needed it for the window decoration,' Jemila said. 'Did you know that you can't get much yarn from the wild plant? Plants like this were created over thousands of years of breeding.'

No, she had not known that.

'You should put it in the display,' Caspia said. 'Although it looks good on the counter as well. You could put a book about cotton next to it.'

'Good idea!' Jemila ran her finger over one of the small fluffy balls. 'How many letters do you have left?'

Caspia let out a deep sigh. 'I opened the last one this morning. Together with my Mom. I tried to wait because we'll be here for quite a while longer. But I just couldn't manage it.'

She pulled the letter from her basket and handed it to Jemila.

Jemila read—and smiled. 'It sounds like this is about my favorite flower.'

'No way! It's Rosalind's favorite flower, too!' Caspia said. 'I've often thought that you two have a lot in common. It is jasmine, right?'

She only realized now that Rosalind would not confirm the answer for her this time.

'Yes, that would be my guess as well.' Jemila let out a deep sigh. 'Ah, Jasmine! A dangerous plant when you're in a romantic mood. But I won't ask any more questions about the boy in the picture.'

'He's just a friend!' Caspia pretended to be studying the

books, so that Jemila could not see her face. 'But I'll warn Laryssa. She's constantly in a romantic mood.'

'That sounds like me!' Jemila sighed again. 'But I usually fall in love with the wrong boys.'

Caspia pulled a book with the title *Witch-Plants and What They Can Really Do* from the shelf. She wasn't sure if she really wanted to talk about love. Although...maybe it was all right with Jemila.

'The boy in the picture is named Ado,' she said. 'He does great drawings. And he's funny. I just like spending time with him. But I don't want to like him too much. After all, I'm only here for a few more weeks!'

'Only a few more weeks? I thought you were staying for a while?' The disappointment in Jemila's voice warmed Caspia's heart.

'Just for the summer. Eleven weeks. I used to think that was an eternity. I really didn't want to come to Brooklyn. But now...'

'...you like it here.' It was not a question.

Caspia felt the truth in Jemila's words like a nettle's burn. Yes. She liked it here. Very much.

'You grew roots,' Jemila observed. 'It's really magical when that happens. You never know where it will be. And it's very difficult tearing them out again.'

'I lived on Saint Lucia for a few years with my mother,' she added when Caspia looked at her questioningly. 'That's an island in the Caribbean. I loved it so much there. The roots just grew. And then my mother suddenly didn't like it anymore and we came back here.'

Jemila shrugged her shoulders. 'This shop helps. And my aunt is a bit gruff, but she understands that I'm homesick. She always says I have to go back there one day.' She pulled back the curtain. 'We got a delivery of jasmine last night. I should have put it in water hours ago, but I was so busy with the herbs.'

She disappeared behind the curtain and Caspia looked through the flower- and book-filled window display to the outside. A bike shot past, and on the other side of a street, a bus was dropping off a wild mixture of passengers. So many different people. Almost as different as Jemila's flowers. Yes, she really did like Brooklyn. But she also missed her home and her friends, her own bed and her things, the quiet of her street at night. How could she love such different places?

You grew roots. It's really magical when that happens. You never know where it will be. And it's very difficult tearing them out again.

When Jemila returned, she was carrying two vases, both filled with flowering vines, one white, one yellow.

'I want to hear more about this boy.' She sat the vases down on the counter. 'But you already said that you don't want the jasmine for romantic reasons. So the yellow one is the one for you.'

Jemila arranged the vines in the vases until they flowed over the whole counter.

'Unfortunately, jasmine is very expensive,' she said and plucked a few wilted blossoms off the thin, firm stems. 'I would have to charge you five dollars for it, otherwise my Zia WILL kill me. But these...' she collected the yellow flowers that had showered off the vines and onto the counter, '...are free! And they smell just as good. When it comes to jasmine it's all about the flowers anyway, isn't it?'

She filled Caspia's cupped hands all the way to the top.

'Yellow jasmine means friendship,' Jemila said. 'And maybe you don't want to hear this, but I don't think you should tell yourself that you're not allowed to like this boy too much. Just because you'll eventually go back home.'

Caspia buried her nose in the yellow flowers that filled her hands. The scent whispered of hot summers and tropical gardens. And of Jemila's friendship.

'Okay. I promise I'll think about it!' she said, carefully pouring the flowers into a small bag that Jemila handed her.

She hesitated for a moment. But then she finally said

what she had been meaning to say for a while now.

'There's a store in Wilmerton, where they sell these small clay fish.' Caspia pulled the pendant out from underneath her T-shirt. 'Ellie, Laryssa and I always wear one around our neck as a symbol of our friendship. I'd like to send you one as well. You don't have to wear it if you don't want to! They don't smell as good as jasmine, but they mean the same thing.'

She turned away just in case tears crept into her eyes. She would miss Jemila terribly. And her store and the flowers and the books. Even the voice of her Zia.

Caspia was already at the door when she turned around once more.

'I'll miss Ado a lot when I go back home. But I think I'll miss you and *Blooms & Books* even more.'

Then she rushed outside because she could really feel the tears coming now. Caspia hated crying. Especially in front of others. Mom had tried to convince her many times that it could feel good to have your heart overflow in front of people who cared for you. But Caspia thought it was just awful. Mom said that even as a little girl Caspia had tried to hold back her tears.

Maybe there was a plant that prevented blushing and the shedding of tears?

An Invitation

Mom wasn't at home when Caspia got back. But she had left her a note. *I am at a class for Caribbean cooking. Tostones! Croquetas de Salmon! Food for you and Dad is on the stove. And jasmine-flavored ice cream is in the freezer. Love, Mom*

Caspia filled a small bowl with water and carefully put the jasmine flowers into it. They looked like tiny water lilies, that floated in the fountain of an equally tiny fairy. The bowl looked really nice between the dandelion and the nasturtium, which was still growing very well—even though a windowsill was not the best place for a garden. That would be much easier in Maine. But Caspia liked her plant window and her delegates of the Green Kingdom.

The jasmine flowers soon filled her room with their fragrance. The Queen of the Night... Caspia laid down on the bed, closed her eyes, and imagined being Rosalind, strolling through a garden in India, with her hands finding blossoms and leaves...

Rosalind...

Caspia sat up. The green ribbon on Minna's grave... It had looked really new. Should she maybe...?

She ate a bowl of jasmine ice cream to give herself courage, before reaching for her computer.

Rosalind Reynolds

She slowly typed the name into the search bar. What if she only found an obituary? Or...nothing...the silence of forgotten things. And people.

But then...

...suddenly there was a link.

LETTERS FROM THE GREEN KINGDOM.
A BLOG ABOUT PLANTS.

She opened the link and her screen turned green. Just a simple, dark green. She heard the rustling of leaves, the humming of insects, bird song...and then a voice. It was the voice of an old woman, but Caspia knew right away that it was Rosalind, even though it was the first time she had heard her speak outside of her letters. As expected, Rosalind had a very beautiful voice. And when she spoke of her love for plants, the screen slowly filled with leaves and flowers as if her voice made them grow. Caspia clicked on one of the blossoms and a letter appeared. It was a riddle! Caspia clicked on another flower, and there was another one. There were dozens! And when she clicked on a small green envelope in the right corner, a text box framed by vines of jasmine appeared.

If you have a question about the Green Kingdom, find a mistake in my riddles, or want to make me aware of a plant I have overlooked so far, feel free to send me an email.

Caspia clicked on a bumblebee and a photo appeared. The old woman smiling at her had untamed white curls and wore glasses with dark lenses. She had the smile of a young girl—the girl whose letters had made Caspia grow roots—in the same city where Rosalind's sister Minna had once lived.

Her heart started to dance and stumble in her chest.

Should she...?

Of course! she heard Ado say. *Of course, my dear*, cried Mrs Wahid, and Jemila raised her eyebrows and asked: *What are you waiting for, Caspia Turkel?*

Caspia took a deep breath.

Dear Mrs Reynolds, she typed.

And deleted it again.

Dear Rosalind, she started over, *my name is Caspia Turkel. My parents and I are spending the summer in Brooklyn, and my father rented the apartment where your sister Minna used to live. Her wallpaper is still there and so is the old dresser where she painted flowers. In one of its drawers I found the ten letters with green riddles that you sent to Minna many years ago. I hope it is all right that I read them. They are really wonderful and I found all of the plants. Thank you so, so much. You have made me an explorer of the Green Kingdom.*

All the very best,
Caspia Turkel

She pressed send before her courage abandoned her. Where did Rosalind live now? She could not find any information about this in her blog. But wait a moment...the email address was from the United Kingdom. That meant—Caspia had to look it up—it was five hours later in England than in Brooklyn! So around midnight. Good. Then it wasn't worth staying in front of her computer and waiting for a reply. Rosalind was probably deeply asleep. And also... it was an email address on a website, not Rosalind's private contact information. With those you usually had to wait for a response for months. IF Rosalind even answered those emails herself rather than someone completely different who had no idea what apartment and what letters Caspia was talking about.

Yes, it was better not to get her hopes up too much!

Caspia closed her laptop.

She still couldn't believe it: she had written to Rosalind!

Ping. That was not an email but a text notification. She reached for her cell phone.

Saturday 11am—community garden
6/15 Green—South Park Slope
(corner 6th Ave & 15th Street)—bring your parents!
Ado

An invitation to a garden? Caspia could not remember Ado ever mentioning this before.

She could hear someone unlock the apartment door.

'I'm back!' Mom called. 'It was so fantastic! I can't wait to make Caribbean food for you and Dad.'

She looked very happy as she poked her head through Caspia's door.

'Ado invited us to a community garden near here. Do you guys want to come?'

'Of course! A community garden AND I will meet the mysterious Ado.'

'Mom!'

'All right. All right, sorry.'

Mom came in and surveyed the windowsill garden.

'The nasturtium is growing really well.' She ran her finger over one of the juicy green leaves. 'Have I ever told you about Benjamin Kothari? He was my best friend when I was your age. We used to watch basketball on TV together and he taught me how to cook. His mother had a restaurant and even back then he could already make the most incredible sauces. I think I was also a bit in love with him. But I only realized that much later.'

So that was the answer to that riddle. Grandma was a seriously bad cook and Caspia had often wondered how her mother learned to cook so well.

We'd love to come, she replied to Ado.

Oh, it would hurt tearing out these roots again.

Sweet Grass

It turned out that Dad had to work all day Saturday.

'I'm really sorry, Cass,' he said. 'We just can't keep up with the work, there's so much to do at the site. But you should see the view! Maybe we can have a picnic up there before we go back home. I'm sure I can convince Jack to allow it.'

That really did sound like an unforgettable adventure. Even if Caspia was sure that she wouldn't be able to get a single bite down that high up. But Brooklyn had made her so much braver, and if Dad was there as well...

Mom shook her head. Absolutely not.

'Mike! Did you forget about the picnic on our tenth wedding anniversary? I threw up before we finished the first glass of champagne! And that scaffolding was only three stories high!'

'But it's completely safe!' Dad tried to soothe her. 'They doubled the safety measures on site after Jack broke his foot!'

Caspia thought that really did sound comforting, but Mom shook her head again. 'If your daughter's that brave, then please! Maybe she got your love of heights from you. I'll prepare you a delicious picnic—and then wave at you from below.'

'All right. That's how we'll do it then!' Dad winked at her and went into the kitchen to pack some of the Caribbean food that Mom had made.

'I've made it a little less spicy,' she called after him.

Last night Caspia and Dad had needed a glass of water after every other bite.

Caspia still felt a slight squeeze in her stomach at the thought of having a picnic on scaffolding so high over the streets of Brooklyn. But she was sure that Jemila and Ado would really like the plan. Mrs Wahid would probably like it as well, but Caspia decided not to tell her anything about it. She could vividly picture how fearlessly Mrs Wahid would scale all the ladders and let her legs dangle at the top. No, it was enough that she climbed the ladder on her old bookshelves. Caspia was sure that Monyet would have agreed with her.

She was very tempted to text Ado to ask what exactly the invitation for Saturday was about. But in the end she decided to let herself be surprised. Instead, she passed the time helping Mom buy all the spices she couldn't get in Maine at Mrs Wahid's shop. She also spent many cozy hours at Blooms & Books helping Jemila reorganize and dust her Zia's books.

Ellie had some really good ideas for new sections. No surprise there. After all, she spent a lot of her time in libraries and bookshops. Jemila painted the flowerpots with symbols for the different sections. A saucepan for edible plants, a fairy for plant myths, a few blossoms for flowers, and an old-fashioned glass vial with a cork stop for healing plants. Caspia was very impressed by how Jemila could create all this with nothing but a paintbrush and a few colors.

It was a lot of work reorganizing so many books, and a few times they stood between the stacks feeling a little lost. But in the end the shelves looked even more beautiful than before, especially thanks to Jemila's painted flowerpots. Finally, Jemila added in some additional fabric flowers. And after that they made butterflies from colorful paper and spread them in front of the books.

‘Good!’ Jemila observed in satisfaction when they both stepped back to admire the result of their sweat-inducing labor.

‘Very good!’ Caspia said.

Jemila’s Zia was not around again because she had gone to see her sister. They had a new system where Jemila texted Caspia as soon as she had the store to herself, but they were both sure that Zia would really like the new organizational scheme.

‘The flowers I painted look a little strange,’ Jemila observed when they sat in the large armchair together sipping jasmine tea. ‘And that pill jar... Hmm... You can’t really tell what that’s supposed to be, can you? Maybe you should have asked Ado to paint us signs.’

But Caspia shook her head firmly. ‘I think your pots are fantastic. You have to paint one for my windowsill garden.’

Jemila was more than happy to do this. She covered it with ladybugs.

Saturday came with blue skies and a fresh breeze—just the right day for a garden visit. Caspia had not heard back anything in response to her email to Rosalind, and she was both disappointed and relieved at the same time. What if she didn’t like Rosalind? What if she was completely different from how she had imagined her? After all, she was very old by now. Yes, it was probably better like this. This way Rosalind would always stay the girl from the letters and her companion to her Brooklyn adventures. And this Saturday belonged to Ado anyway!

Caspia had never been to a community garden... There was no such thing in Maine—as far as she knew.

'Well, most people have a backyard where we live,' said Mom, when they headed out. 'Community gardens make more sense in a city where most people don't have their own backyard but would like to have a few beds where they can plant vegetables or their own flowers.'

That made sense. But why did Ado want to meet there and not at the BBG? And why did he want her to bring her parents?

The gate to the community garden looked very inviting. The sign and the posts were painted with flowers, making it feel like you had discovered an enchanted garden in the middle of the city. For a moment Caspia thought she had written down the wrong address. Half a dozen tables were set up among the flower beds humming with bees. They were decorated with flowers and covered with colorful plates and bowls with all sorts of dishes. It all looked a lot like a family meet-up or a party for the garden community.

Caspia was hesitating by the gate when she heard Ado's voice.

'Surprise!' he cried. 'You can all come out! They're here!'

The garden was full of laughing faces. They appeared from behind the trees, the beanstalks, and the sunflowers. There was Mrs Wahid with two small children at her side, and Jemila with a woman who Caspia suspected was her aunt. Even Margaret from the Botanic Garden was there and

Ado's father stepped out of a small shed.

'When you said you had found new friends, I didn't expect so many,' Mom whispered as she surveyed the many different foods with delight.

'I didn't know there were so many either,' Caspia replied and smiled at Ado.

How had he even known about them all? *Probably from you*, she could hear Laryssa say. *Whenever you like a boy, he soon knows everything about you.*

'Do you like it?' Ado asked. 'My uncle has a few beds here and I thought it would be a nice place for a Caspia-is-growing-roots-in-Brooklyn party.'

He shook Mom's hand. 'It's nice to meet you, Mrs Turkel.'

Caspia had not known he could be so formal. He even wore a white shirt and a tie. Although it had green parrots printed on it.

Oh, she really did like Ado a lot.

Jemila liked him too. *He's as nice as I thought he would be*, said her smile when she and her aunt appeared next to Ado.

'It took quite a bit of detective work to find us all,' she whispered to Caspia. 'But Ado is a very good detective. And I can finally introduce you to my Zia. Aunt Loretta,' she said with her voice slightly raised. 'This is Caspia, the girl who distracts me from work so much because she's always searching for some plant.'

Caspia had pictured Jemila's Zia completely differently—kind of old with broad shoulders and a little scary. But her aunt Loretta was still pretty young and very tall and thin. Her curly gray hair was as short as Mom's and her broad smile reminded Caspia of Jemila's.

'I hear that you like my books,' she said.

'And your flowers,' said Caspia. 'Do you like the way we reorganized the books?'

'Very much,' Loretta said. 'I have to admit Jemila has made my store much more exciting since she started helping me. And it sounds like you did your share as well. Even though you two...'

'Anna?' she called and waved. 'It's me! Loretta from the Caribbean cooking class!'

Caspia's Mom waved back.

'She made the dishes even better than our teacher!' she said to Jemila and Caspia.

Then she headed toward Caspia's mother and the two of them began talking about recipes.

'My Zia knows your mother, who would have thought?' Jemila whispered. 'It's like I always say. Brooklyn is a village! Have you heard from Rosalind yet?'

Caspia shook her head. 'I'm not even sure if she reads those emails herself. After all, I only have the email address on that website.'

Ado brought over two glasses of lemonade for them.

'He's so polite,' Jemila whispered, when his uncle called him over. 'And nice. You have much better taste than me when it comes to boys.'

Caspia was sure that the color of her face perfectly matched the tomatoes that grew all around them.

'There she is, boys!' Mrs Wahid beamed at Caspia. 'Caspia, the plant finder!'

The two little boys holding her hands looked up at Caspia suspiciously.

'She is a princess from the Green Kingdom,' said Mrs Wahid. 'And she was born from a peapod, far, far away from here, up in the north of Maine. Monyet also likes her a lot.'

This seemed to surprise her grandsons even more than the peapod.

Caspia took many pictures that afternoon. With Mrs Wahid, Ado and Jemila, Ado's father and his uncle and Margaret, who had brought her boyfriend.

'Maybe my fiancé,' she whispered to Caspia.

Oh, Caspia loved the *Caspia-is-growing-roots-in-Brooklyn Party!*

She was just sad that her dad could not be there to meet all of her friends. But there was still his idea of the picnic high above the city. As expected, Jemila and Ado both thought the idea of sitting on scaffolding high over the city was very exciting.

'Of course! We can do it on the evening before you leave,' Ado suggested. 'What could be a better farewell to Brooklyn than seeing it from above? We won't even have a chance to be sad!'

'Exactly!' Jemila confirmed and started surveying the buildings that surrounded the garden. She was probably counting the floors. Caspia had done the same. None of them had ten.

'We still have a small surprise for you. Something you can take back to Maine with you.' Ado looked around, searching. 'I wonder if she made it. Mrs Mehegan?' he called.

A woman gently pushed past Mrs Wahid's grandchildren. She had her long gray hair in braids like a young girl and held a large bunch of dried grass in her hands.

'Ado told me that you like plants and maybe don't know this one yet,' she said, as she put the bunch of grass into Caspia's arms. 'It's sweet grass and brings luck and good health.'

'Mrs Mehegan is a good friend of my mother's,' Ado

explained. 'And can you believe it? She was also a close friend of Minna Reynolds!'

Mrs Mehegan smiled at Caspia. 'I heard that you found some letters from Rosalind in Minna's old flower dresser. Minna's daughter and I must have missed them when we cleaned out her things.'

She waved over a little girl who was watching the wasps and bees swarming around the flowers. 'Jeannie! Bring me that bag I gave you. And stay away from those wasps!'

Jeannie was obviously not very concerned about their stings. She turned away reluctantly. But then she ran toward Mrs Mehegan and handed her the bag that was slung over her shoulder.

'Minna made this for some green riddle game of her sister's,' said Mrs Mehegan, as she pulled a green velvet pouch out of her bag. 'Minna's daughter, Willow, is also a passionate embroiderer, that's why Rosalind gave her these after Minna's death. But maybe you'd like to solve the riddles as well? Willow would be happy to lend them to you.'

She pulled a stack of cards from the pouch.

And there they were. Minna's green riddles. The cards that Mrs Mehegan handed Caspia were the size of postcards but made of much thicker stock, and on each was a piece of cloth embroidered with a plant. Caspia ran her fingers over the delicate stitches, which formed a sprig of rosemary.

'Minna always said that her sister's blindness gave her a passion for embroidery,' said Mrs Mehegan. 'She moved to Brooklyn because she fell in love with a boy who was from here. Later she married him and had Willow. Minna was such a good embroiderer that she worked for theaters and fashion houses, and when she and Willow's father got divorced, she even opened her own store. Unfortunately, it doesn't exist anymore. Willow took it over for a while, but then she moved to Chicago.'

The second card showed sea holly. Caspia closed her eyes and followed the prickly stem with her fingers up to the violet flower. Oh yes, Rosalind must have loved these cards.

'Mrs Mehegan has also met Rosalind a few times,' Ado said as if he had read her mind.

'Of course!' Mrs Mehegan confirmed. 'She used to come at least once a year to visit her sister! Rosalind never married. Minna used to tease her saying she was too picky because she turned down more than one proposal. But Rosalind loved her freedom more than anything else. Well, except her sister perhaps. And her plants. And she is still a keen world traveler.'

Caspia pulled another card from the pouch. She had no idea what the plant on it was called. Oh, this would be a lot of fun! And this time her parents would work them out with her.

'Hello, hello,' Jemila called. 'The wasps are well on their way to devouring our food. Let's steal at least a few bites from them!'

Everybody was happy to rise to the occasion. The dishes waiting on the tables were as varied as the flowers and vegetables that grew in the beds around them. Mrs Wahid had prepared Indonesian food. Jemila and her aunt had cooked something Caribbean, which Mom was especially enthusiastic about. Margaret had made Swedish pancakes, and Ado's father proudly revealed a plate of tostadas that Ado's mother had made even though she had to be at their youngest son's soccer game that afternoon.

The setting sun was already filling the garden with shadows when everybody began packing up the remaining food and collecting paper plates and cups for the compost. Caspia liked the idea that the leftovers of this unforgettable day would soon help flowers and lettuces grow.

'So...a ton of new plants to figure out!' said Ado as his father carried the last table back to his uncle's pickup truck. Everybody else had left already. Margaret and her maybe-fiancé, Mrs Mehegan, Jemila and her Zia, Mrs Wahid and her grandsons...

'Yes, there are eight cards!' Caspia said. 'And I have a few more weeks to track them all down in Brooklyn.'

Ado noticed that there was a touch of sadness in her voice. 'Exactly! We still have a few weeks left. And Maine isn't all that far away.'

He hugged her, long and tight.

'We'll manage,' he said. 'Maybe we can write letters? Even though my spelling is pretty bad!'

'Mine too.' Caspia laughed. But she liked the idea of writing Ado letters. And finding one of his in her mailbox in Wilmerton.

'You really have very nice friends,' Mom said as they made their way back. 'How did you find them all in such a short time?'

Caspia buried her face in the sweet grass that Mrs Mehegan had brought. 'The plants,' she said. 'They taught me to put down roots.'

High Above the Roofs

So there it was. Her last evening in Brooklyn. Her dad's friend had not cared much for their plan of a picnic on the scaffolding. But Caspia's dad was very good at convincing people. He could even argue with Grandma and win her over to his point of view—something neither Mom nor Caspia had ever managed to do.

'Because he looks so innocent and friendly!' Mom always said. 'But in reality, your father is as cunning as a fox and as roguish as a badger.'

The scaffolding turned out to be very high. Even higher than Caspia had expected. But there were railings and ropes everywhere and Dad made sure that no one climbed on the ladders that led to less secure spots, even though Jemila was sorely tempted.

Caspia was surprised by how easy it was to look down as long as she could feel the other three beside her. There was no end to all the surprising things that she was learning about herself and the world. You could really become addicted to it.

She sat down in a spot where she could let her legs dangle through the railings and see all the way to Jamaica Bay, as Dad had described so many times. He had bought bagels and brownies, three hot chocolates, and a coffee for himself. And there they sat, high above Brooklyn—well, not high above all of Brooklyn, but a large part of it—and Caspia thought: *More! More adventures! More places!* But first and foremost, more friendships. That was the best spice in the soup. Brooklyn had taught her that. And Rosalind.

'Still no reply from her?' Ado asked.

Caspia shook her head. 'No, but it's all right.'

And it was. In this moment, everything was all right. As Ado had predicted, this was a good way to say goodbye. They had solved all of Minna's embroidered riddles and found all of the plants she had stitched. It had been teamwork: Ellie, Laryssa, Jemila, Ado, and herself had taken turns to come up with five clues for each of Minna's plants, just like Rosalind had done in her letters. Mom and Dad had also helped to work them out.

It was Ellie who realized that the first letters of the plants on Minna's cards spelled out Rosalind's name—if you arranged them in the right order. Caspia really would have liked to have a sister like Minna.

But now it was time to go home.

'What kind of houses do they build in Maine, Mr Turkel?' asked Ado.

Dad shrugged his shoulders. 'I have to admit, they're not very exciting. But I think the last few weeks have made us all a little more adventurous. So, when we get back I'll buy a boat.'

Caspia almost choked on her hot chocolate. 'A boat?'

All right, their house was full of model ships that her father had built—they were terrible at gathering dust as Grandma never got tired of pointing out. But a full-size, real-life boat?

'Cool,' Ado said. 'I've always wanted to have a boat.'

'We had one on St Lucia,' said Jemila. 'Very small, but it was a good boat. It was red.'

Caspia looked out over Jamaica Bay. A boat! So, Dad also had dreams, which she knew nothing about. Although... with his passion for model ships, he really hadn't been hiding it. She had just never thought to ask why he loved building small ships so much.

Dad put his arm around her shoulders. 'Don't look so surprised,' he said. 'Boats are a bit like houses. You just build them so they can swim, but, other than that, they're not so different. They're houses that can travel. And didn't you want to go visit a cinnamon tree? And Indian gardens that smell like jasmine?'

Was he serious?

He looked like he was serious. 'During the last few months, I've looked down on Jamaica Bay every day,' he said. 'I think all the glittering water reminded me that as a child I spent more time on a boat than on firm ground, because my father loved watching all the birds that live down by the river. We often headed out before the sun had even come up. Crakes, king rails, grouse... I could name them all. Have I really never told you about that?'

Caspia shook her head.

'Well, that's why I'm going to buy a boat when we're back home,' said Dad. 'And because I've always wanted one. An old boat that I can restore.'

That sounded like a very different adventure from Brooklyn. But that was probably the point of adventures: that there was always something new and different about them?

'What does Mom think about the idea?'

'She thinks I'm ridiculous. But she likes my wild side.'

Caspia smiled. Yes, she did.

'I'll come visit you to check out the boat,' said Jemila. 'After all, I lived on an island for many years!'

'I'll come too,' said Ado. 'So the boat can't be too small, so we can all fit.'

'I'll keep that in mind,' said Dad, and they all looked down at the shimmering water of Jamaica Bay.

'I wonder which trees make the best wood for boats,' said Caspia.

'Good question. We should find out,' said Dad.

Ado pulled out his cell phone.

'Damn,' he murmured. 'No service.'

A Surprise in the Evening

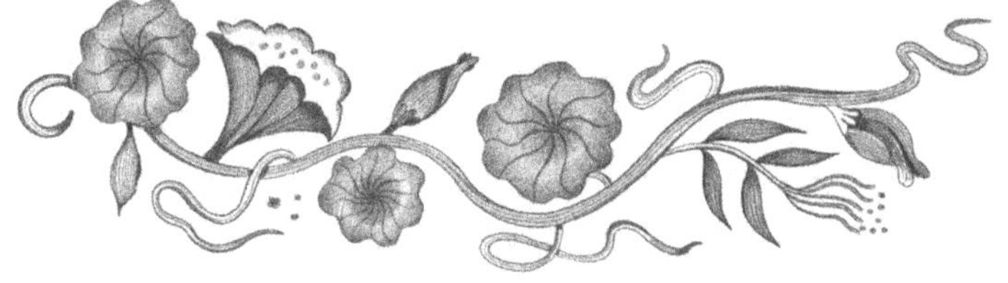

Two months later, Dad was back at his old company and working on houses that were only one or two stories tall. But he had rented an overgrown bit of land down by the river with a shabby little boat house. And he had bought an old boat that he worked on every weekend.

Sometimes Caspia helped him, but she missed Brooklyn. Laryssa and Ellie agreed that she definitely talked about it way too much—and that they also definitely wanted to visit. All the plants from Caspia's windowsill had made it to Maine unscathed, and the dandelion now grew in the garden next to the thistle and the butterfly weed that Dad had rescued at the construction site. But Maine was too cold for the tomato plant that Ado had given Caspia as a farewell gift, so that stood on the windowsill in her room. It was too late for fruit but Caspia had high hopes for the spring.

Brooklyn tomatoes! Or did the water and the soil now make Ado's plant a Maine tomato?

I would call it a BrookMaine or a MainLyn tomato, Ado texted when Caspia asked him. They texted each other often. And there was still the group chat with Jemila. Unfortunately, Mrs Wahid was not one for text chats. But Caspia had already sent her a postcard.

Mom had finished her cookbook. She called it *Recipes from the Green Kingdom* and had told Grandma that only positive comments were welcome. A rule that Grandma had surprisingly managed to follow so far.

It was a cold, rainy day. Mom was in the kitchen cleaning mushrooms, which she had foraged from the forest, and Laryssa and Ellie had come over to despair over their math homework together when there was a knock at the door.

Caspia was sure that it would be Grandma, wanting to suggest a recipe for Mom's cookbook as she wasn't allowed to criticize it anymore. But when Caspia opened the door with a sigh, an old woman stood in front of it who was definitely not her grandmother. She wore glasses with round dark lenses and her unruly curls were as white as the blossoms of a dog rose.

'I hope you are having a wonderful evening,' she said. 'Would you let me hear your voice, so that I can tell whether you're Caspia or her mother? Or maybe her father?'

It was impossible, wasn't it?

How had she found her?

'Hello, Rosalind,' Caspia barely managed to get out.

'Ah, I guessed correctly!' Rosalind smiled just as Caspia had always imagined. 'Please forgive me for not having responded to your email yet, but I was on the other side of the world. I only just returned to these shores, to visit a wonderful tree a little further up the coast. When I remembered that Mrs Mehegan had told me that the girl who had brought her Minna's letters lived in Maine, *Rosalind*, I said to myself, *Caspia Turkel would surely like to see this tree as well. Why don't you get her address from Mrs Mehegan and invite her to visit it with you?*'

Caspia smiled.

Of course, Rosalind had come for that. To introduce her to a tree. After all, that's how it had all begun.

'Who's there, Caspia?' Mom called from the kitchen.

Ellie and Laryssa emerged at the living room door and stared at the strange woman talking to Caspia.

'That's...' Laryssa began.

'The blind girl!' cried Ellie.

'Well, not a girl anymore!' said Rosalind and laughed out loud. 'But you two still are, based on your voices. And I smell delicious food. I heard a lot about the culinary talents of your mother back in Brooklyn.'

'Really?' Mom stood in the kitchen door, a mushroom in her hand.

'Oh yes, Brooklyn is a village!' said Rosalind. 'Sooner or later everyone knows everything about everyone! At least that's what my sister always said.'

Mom smiled. 'Today I'm cooking something that was inspired by your letters. Would you like to be our guest of honor?'

It turned into a magical dinner. And not just because of Mom's wild mushroom ragout, which tasted just as good in Maine as it had in Brooklyn. When Dad got home, Rosalind noticed that he smelled of boat wax. And so they spoke of traveling, of cinnamon plantations, and whether you could really sail from Maine to Indonesia. Dad and Rosalind agreed that it was probably an impossible endeavor after all. But Rosalind had a thousand other ideas for amazing-sounding boat adventures.

'What kind of a tree is it?' Caspia whispered, when Mom went into the kitchen to get dessert. 'The one we're visiting?'

'Oh, that's a surprise, of course!' Rosalind whispered back. 'But I will give you a clue: back in the day, women used to throw its fruit into the fire, to find out who would be the next to marry.'